Friendships

Friendships

Avoiding the Ones That Hurt, Finding the Ones That Heal

Jeff Wickwire

Chosen

Grand Rapids, Michigan

Published by Chosen Books
A division of Baker Publishing Group
P.O. Box 6287, Grand Rapids, MI, 49516-6287
www.chosenbooks.com

Printed in the United States of America

Library of Congress Cataloging-in-Publication Data
Wickwire, Jeff.
    Friendships : avoiding the ones that hurt, finding the ones that heal / Jeff Wickwire.
        p.   cm.
    ISBN 10: 0-8007-9427-3 (pbk.)
    ISBN 978-0-8007-9427-9 (pbk.)
    1. Friendship—Religious aspects—Christianity. 2. Interpersonal rela-tions—Religious aspects—Christianity. I. Title
    BV4647.F7W535 2007
    241'.6762—dc22   2007003901

To George and Gerry
Your encouragement and support through the years has
lifted me to reach for the best.

To Beverly
You are a true friend. We thank you.

And finally, to my mother
You are rich in friends with more than most! Thank you
for your love and prayers.

CONTENTS

7

Contents

Part 4 Cleavers

"So help me GOD—not even death itself is going to come between us!"—Ruth 1:17

Acknowledgments

Every author needs that first break in publishing. My heartfelt thanks goes to Jane Campbell of Chosen Books for taking that risk with me. Now, three books later, she remains a friend and encourager, still willing to publish the messages God puts on my heart.

A special thanks to editor Melanie Johnson; the staff of Chosen, including Jessica Miles, Karen Steele and Katy Pent; and everyone else who helped make this book a reality.

To Kristine Christlieb, for solid suggestions and editing.

And to Cathy, my greatest fan. I am *her* greatest fan.

INTRODUCTION

Last night I woke up with an old song playing in my head. It was the classic originally written and sung by Carole King, then picked up by James Taylor. Yup, you guessed it; "You've Got a Friend" came drifting into my dreams. The lyrics are powerfully true and capture the essence of what this book is about. The song is beautiful in its simplicity, and I feel the warmth of friendship like a soft crackling fire on a cold winter night oozing from its words: "Winter, spring, summer, or fall, all you have to do is call. . . ."

I lay awake for a good hour thinking about those lyrics. Why did they stick like old graffiti on the walls of my mind after all these years? Because like all great songs, "You've Got a Friend" strikes a nerve, a place of truth deep within. We all want and need friends. Like the old porch light left burning on a harsh winter night, a true friend beckons us out of the cold to a place of safety and comfort.

Through time and experience, it has dawned on me as never before the crucial role friends play in our lives. The friends we make will decide much of what we become in terms of character and spiritual depth, or the lack thereof. I have also been delightfully surprised at how often Scripture addresses the issue of friends. Contrary to what many may think, it is hardly silent on the subject. Filled with encouragements, warnings, insights and riveting stories, the Bible leaves no stone unturned on this crucial topic.

This book is not a how-to manual. I do not deal, per se, with how to make friends, become more popular and so on. Rather, I have attempted to take an honest look at some of the pitfalls, disappointments and heartbreaks of friendship, as well as the anatomy of true friendship, what it looks like, what it is comprised of and what the characteristics that make it endure are. I have also attempted to cut through the gullibility bubble that often surrounds all things Christian in order to frankly discuss the reality of friendship within the Christian world.

My prayer is that the friendships in your life will be enriched through this book, and that the greatest Friend of all (about whom much of that song could have been written) will become more real to you than ever before. Indeed, if you are at this moment lonely and "friendless," you've still got a Friend.

PART 1

THE AWESOME POWER OF FRIENDSHIP

"Friendship is the greatest of worldly goods. Certainly to me it is the chief happiness of life."

—C. S. Lewis[1]

"If you live to be 100, I want to live to be 100 minus one day, so I never have to live without you."

—Winnie the Pooh

1

A Friend-Shaped Hole
in Every Soul

The righteous should choose his friends carefully.

Proverbs 12:26, NKJV

As a pastor and host of a daily radio program, I regularly witness the high-level importance people place on relationships. It is a very hot topic. Each time I speak about maintaining healthy, godly friendships, it strikes a deep vein in the listeners. Recently, when I brought several talks on the radio about friendship, our ministry was literally flooded with orders for the teaching series. Others drove miles just to visit our church and purchase what they had heard on the radio program. Why? *We are designed to enjoy an intimate relationship with God and are called by Christ into healthy relationship with others.* "These things I command you, that ye love one another" (John 15:17, KJV). Living a happy, blessed and productive life hinges on our ability to maintain successful relationships: vertically (with God) and horizontally (with our fellow man).

Jesus was crystal clear on this matter. We cannot love and serve God properly if our friendships are out of whack. Have you felt the pressure? I am sure that you have dealt with a friendship issue at one time or another and will agree—hands down—that friendships can open the doors to much joy and fulfillment in our lives, but they can also bring many questions and conflicts. Friendships are absolutely relevant in our walk with God. We are hardwired to relate to others. God has placed a "friend-shaped" hole in every soul.

God Cares about Your Friends

No one wields the power of influence over you more than your friends. Where you are in life five years from now will depend primarily on two things: the strength of your commitment to God and who your friends are.

Take a close look at those to whom you have extended the hand of friendship, because many of their habits and attitudes will likely become yours. The lens through which they see life will—in important, substantive ways—also become your lens. Noted speaker W. Clement Stone warns, "Be careful the environment you choose, for it will shape you; be careful the friends you choose, for you will become like them."[1] Show me who you are running with and I will have met *you*.

Positive friendships can sharpen your character, strengthen your dreams and help carry you through your darkest hours. Michael W. Smith put it so well in song: "Friends are friends forever if the Lord's the Lord of them."[2] Conversely, bad friendships can be the means through which you plummet to the depths of degradation and lose your spiritual walk, your dreams and your self-worth.

The Bible reveals that who your friends are matters very much to God! The words *friend, friends, friendly* and *friendship* are found *107 times in twenty different books of the Bible.* As one who decided long ago to become a fully devoted disciple of Jesus Christ, I am more convinced than ever that as your friendships go, so goes your spiritual life. The two cannot be separated.

Staying Alive

Everyone needs friends. Without them the world is like a cold glacier drifting through an ocean of emptiness. Think about it. One of the first things to cross our minds upon waking to a new day is what we will do with our friends. Friends make the places and experiences of our lives meaningful. Who wants to go to the mall, the fair, church—or anywhere for that matter—alone? While we all need a certain amount of solitude for personal reflection and down time, we need friends to bring our lives to life. An old rock song woefully wailed: "One is the loneliest number that you'll ever do."[3] People do not like lonely. People like friends.

Unfortunately, America has become a very lonely nation. "Americans are far more socially isolated today than they were two decades ago," reports a recent article in the *Washington Post.* "A quarter of Americans say they have no one with whom they can discuss personal troubles; this is more than double the number who were similarly isolated in 1985."[4]

Even the medical and professional communities agree on the importance of close friendships. One national survey found, "Three-quarters of the adult population said that having close, personal friendships was a top priority."[5] Many in the psychiatric community now believe friendship is directly linked to good health.

Another study confirms that friendships could prolong life.[6] Nearly 1,500 people over seventy years of age were asked how much personal and phone contact they had with various social networks, including children, relatives, friends and confidants (including spouses). The group was

17

monitored annually for the first four years of the study and afterward about every three years.

Surprisingly, after ten years of follow-up, researchers found that close contact with children and relatives had little impact on the risk of death. However, a strong network of friends and confidants significantly reduced the risk of death during the follow-up period. The older adults with the strongest network of friends were 22 percent less likely to die during the study than those with the weakest network of good friendships. Researchers have concluded that in times of difficulty friends may exert a healthy influence on potentially risky behaviors like smoking and drinking, as well as have important effects on mood, self-esteem and coping.

General Ulysses S. Grant had just such a faithful friend. John A. Rawlins was closer to Grant than any other person throughout the Civil War. It was to Rawlins that Grant pledged to abstain from drinking. When he broke that pledge, Rawlins pleaded with him for his own sake, and the sake of the nation, to stop drinking. Grant listened.

If you visit the Capitol in Washington, D.C., you will see in front the magnificent monument of General Grant, sitting on his horse in a heroic pose, flanked on either side by stirring battle scenes. But at the other end of Pennsylvania Avenue, a bit to the south, is Rawlins Park, where a very ordinary statue of Grant's true friend, John Rawlins, stands. When you look at Grant's statue, you cannot help but think of this one, the statue of the man who kept Grant on that horse.[7]

We need God and we need healthy, supportive friendships in order to survive and thrive.

Two Kinds of Friends

There are two Greek words for "friend" in the New Testament. The first word, *philos* (fee'-los), refers to having personal affection, attachment, sentiment or feeling for

18

someone.[8] In Scripture, *philos* is used to refer to a true friend. It is a term of endearment. For instance, Jesus said to His disciples, "Our friend [*philos*] Lazarus sleeps, but I go that I may wake him up" (John 11:11, NKJV).

Conversely, the apostle James warned, "Whoever therefore wants to be a friend [*philos*] of the world makes himself an enemy of God" (James 4:4, NKJV). So beware! If you make the world your friend, you will be pulled away from God's best for your life through unwise attractions and attachments. It is entirely possible to harbor an excessive affection for the world that hinders your walk with God. (Much more on this in chapter 12.)

The second word for "friend," *hetairos* (het-ah'-ee-ros), refers to a more shallow, less emotionally involved sentiment.[9] Americans would use the word *acquaintance* or *buddy* to express this same thought. When Judas betrayed Jesus with a kiss, Christ said to him, "Friend [*hetairos*], do what you came for" (Matthew 26:50, NIV). This was a very telling statement. Judas, like the other disciples, had walked with Jesus for several years—he even kept track of the money—yet Jesus called him an *acquaintance*. In every other place where Christ referred to His disciples as "friends," He used the stronger term of endearment. What does this tell us? It is entirely possible to be in the presence of Christ, surrounded by His works, while still keeping your heart at a distance from God. In this book we will focus on the *philos* kind of friend, those for whom we have personal attachments and whom we hold in godly affection.

Friends at Crossroads

One friendship stands out as having been a defining hallmark for me. It came about at the juncture of the most important transition of my life: my journey from death to life in Christ.

I can still remember vividly the weeks and months following my initial commitment to follow Christ in total discipleship. I was in my late teens and hugely excited about what
had taken place in my life. At the outset of my decision, God
gave me a new best friend. In fact, it was the same person who
had invited me to the Bible study where I made my decision.
Night after night, Chuck and I would sit up until the wee
hours of the morning discussing everything that mattered to
two guys in their late teens. Spiritual issues, Bible questions,
girls, our future, different Christian leaders, sexual purity,
God's purpose for us; no stone was left unturned.

Looking back, I can see how important it was in those
formative years to have a sounding board, someone before
whom I could lay all my cards on the table. There was nothing I was afraid to bring up to Chuck and vice versa. It was
a comfort to know that I was not "weird" when it came to
some of the issues I had to work through. More than one
night, kicked back in stuffed chairs, lazily plucking through
some new song with our guitars, I would work up the courage to bring up an issue that was bothering me.

One night I blurted out the question, "Do you think God
has 'the one' in terms of who you marry? Does He, like, point
to someone and command you to marry her?" This had
become a concern of mine because this particular teaching
had been floating around our circle, and it was spooking me.
"I know!" Chuck blurted out. "That's been bugging me, too!
Because what if He told you to marry so and so, or, even
worse, so and so?" We stood up, shuddered, shook, had a
great laugh and poof! Instantly, the weight was gone. Not
that we came up with any answers; it was just the awareness
that I was not alone in my varying struggles that brought
peace and assurance to my heart.

Friends can do that. When you open up to a friend, you
know that no matter what you say, it will pass through
the soft filter of someone who knows who you really are
and loves you anyway. How about you? What treasured

20

experiences have been enriched even more by the precious, godly friends in your life? Take a moment and thank God for authentic *philos* relationships, for they are one of the means by which God releases His priceless anointing and unfathomable blessing into your life.

> How wonderful, how beautiful, when brothers and sisters get along! It's like costly anointing oil flowing down head and beard, flowing down Aaron's beard, flowing down the collar of his priestly robes. It's like the dew on Mount Hermon flowing down the slopes of Zion. Yes, that's where GOD commands the blessing, ordains eternal life.
>
> Psalm 133:1–3

Birds of a Feather

The friendships we keep are very accurate thermometers of our own spiritual condition. Someone having a lukewarm relationship with Christ will gravitate toward and attract lukewarm friends. A person with a backslidden heart will gather with birds of the same feather every time. In the same vein, red-hot, fervent faith will likewise draw a kindred spirit. If you want to know the level of a person's commitment to God, you need look no further than his or her closest friends. (Psst! That is a hint to you if you are looking for a permanent mate. *Start* by checking out his or her friends first.)

I noticed early on in working with young people that two rebels could be placed on opposite sides of a large crowd and find each other in five minutes, as if guided by radar. It was uncanny. Conversely, the kids who were turned on for Christ invariably connected with others of strong faith. *Similar attitudes attract.*

The effect friends can have on us for bad or good is awesome. One of the great proverbs on friendship says, "As iron sharpens iron, so a man sharpens the countenance of

21

his friend" (Proverbs 27:17, NKJV). The word *countenance* means "the look on someone's face."[10] Have you ever noticed that the people you hang out with eventually affect the look on your face? Positive, fulfilling friendships sculpt a look of joy, peace and strength on our countenance, while bad friendships can etch out a hard, bitter, unhappy and downcast expression. You can tell a lot about someone's close associates by the look on his or her face.

This is especially true with teenagers. The moment they begin to associate with rebellious, angry friends, their countenances change. This is no revelation for you if you have a teenage son or daughter. I have personally watched the countenances of teens morph overnight from expressions of peace and contentment to the hard, angry looks of disgruntled rebels. No matter how you shake it, God is making sure that we understand this: Our friends have a power over us matched by little else. We might restate Proverbs 27:17 this way, "As iron sharpens iron, so a man helps chisel out the look on the face of his friend."

> WHETHER WE REALIZE IT OR NOT, THE WAYS OF OUR FRIENDS INFLUENCE OUR BEHAVIOR AND OUR OUTLOOK ON LIFE.

The *Ways* of Friends

Another example of the awesome influence of a friend is found in Proverbs 22:24–25, "Make no friendship with an angry man, and with a furious man do not go, lest you learn his ways and set a snare for your soul" (NKJV). The Hebrew word from which we get "ways" means "way of life, manner of conduct."[11] The way we conduct ourselves transfers to others in a close friendship. Likewise, we take on the *ways* of our closest friends. Whether we realize it or not, the *ways* of our friends influence our behavior and our outlook on life.

22

This same dynamic works in our vertical relationship with God. Isaiah 55:6, 8–9 declares, "Seek the LORD while he may be found; call on him while he is near. . . . 'For . . . as the heavens are higher than the earth, so are my ways higher than your ways and my thoughts than your thoughts'" (NIV). When we seek God and draw close to Him, His *ways* and thoughts become our own. Jesus said to His disciples, "You are My friends if you do whatever I command you" (John 15:14, NKJV). Jesus knew that *His ways* would become *their ways* by virtue of maintaining a close relationship with Him.

> IF THE WAYS OF YOUR FRIENDS ARE UNGODLY, YOU CAN BECOME SNARED IN THE SAME WAY THEY ARE.

Ways are more caught than taught. We catch the ways our friends respond to stress and temptation, and how they make crucial life choices.

Language, habits and attitudes toward God are all part of the *ways* of friends. Make no mistake: *If the ways of your friends are ungodly, you can become snared in the same way they are.* If their manner of conduct is godly, you will likewise learn their ways, and these friendships will bring a blessing to your soul. Remember Solomon's warning again from Proverbs 12:26, "The righteous should choose his friends carefully, for the way of the wicked leads them astray" (NKJV).

Four Levels of Friendship

Generally speaking, there are four levels of friendship:

Acquaintances
Casual friendships
Close friendships
Intimate friendships (best friends)

Acquaintances

An acquaintance is a person with whom you have only occasional contact. This could include someone you meet at the store or a person whom you hire to paint your house. I love to play tennis and racquetball. Through the years, I have met many people in that context with whom I played only once or twice. They were acquaintances. With acquaintances there are no emotional strings attached and no risk in terms of emotional vulnerability. This is why Jesus' words to Judas in Matthew 26:50 were so stunning. Judas had walked with Jesus for years—watching Him heal the sick, raise the dead and teach the Scriptures with absolute authority and power—yet Judas did not invest himself in the relationship. There is a difference between spending time with someone and investing in a relationship. Acquaintances may spend some of their time with you, but they rarely invest it.

Casual Friendships

A casual friendship is based on common interests or activities. If you hit it off at the acquaintance level, things may progress to a casual friendship. This level of friendship goes beyond the "How's the weather?" mode. Activities are planned together, occasional phone calls are made, and light, happy talks about superficial things are common. Invariably, though, this level of friendship does not hold much commitment or emotional loyalty. It is based primarily on the superficial touch points of life that do not require a real level of depth or transparency with another.

Close Friendships

Acquaintance and casual level friendships will not satisfy the deep need we all have to truly know and to be known—this can only happen in deeper relationships. In these final days of history about which the Bible warns that "the love of many shall wax cold" (Matthew 24:12, KJV), we Christians are exhorted to maintain healthy, nurturing relationships.

> Let's see how inventive we can be in encouraging love and helping out, not avoiding worshiping together as some do but spurring each other on, especially as we see the big Day approaching.
>
> Hebrews 10:24–25

In a close friendship there exists a far greater level of transparency and trust. The superficial walls we place around ourselves for protection begin to come down. We feel far more comfortable opening up about conflicts, temptations, marriage issues, kids, doubts, fears, etc. It is our close friends whom we call in a moment of crisis. When a marriage dissolves, the kids get into trouble, we lose a job or we receive a bad report from the doctor, we know a close friend will be there to lend a helping hand. Without close friendships the world can be a very cold and lonely place.

Intimate Friendships (Best Friends)

Best friends are close friends squared. Best friends are the closest things to sibling bonds on earth—sometimes closer (see Proverbs 18:24). You will not have many best friends. As the old saying goes, if you have two best friends at the end of your life, you are rich. Your best friend knows your deepest secrets and holds them safely in the vault of loyalty. An intimate friendship is based on strong transparency and vulnerability (*I will never hurt you*), accountability (*I will allow you to speak into my life*) and a commitment to the development of each other's character and potential (*I want the very best for you*).

A best friend can tell by the sound of your voice or a fleeting facial expression that something is wrong or right. Best friends pull one another out of the ditch of failure without the slightest raised eyebrow, judgment or rejection. *Intimate friends walk in when others walk out.* Whether you have mud on your face or have to eat crow over an embarrassing mistake, "friends love through all kinds of weather" (Proverbs 17:17).

Abraham Lincoln, a well-documented melancholic, who fought all of his life against dark depression, often leaned on the strength of friends to help pull him through an episode. During one particularly bad spell, when the future president actually spoke of suicide, his best friend, Joshua Speed, "had to remove razors from his room—take away all knives and other such dangerous things."[12] Speed finally faced his friend as only a friend can and told him that he would "die unless he rallied."[13]

The somber words and support of a loving friend pulled Lincoln through his crisis. It was following this intervention from his trusted associate that an "irrepressible desire" to accomplish something while he lived crystallized in Lincoln's mind. It is difficult to imagine what America would be like had Lincoln not been able to rely upon a true friend in his midnight hour. Can you imagine what your life would be like without a true, trusted and godly friend?

Unequally Yoked

While friends are necessary to our growth as human beings, the Bible is very clear about what kinds of friendships those professing faith in Christ should have. Scripture teaches that acquaintances and casual friendships with those not embracing the Christian faith cannot and should not be avoided. The apostle Paul penned the following commonsense words of wisdom:

I wrote you in my earlier letter that you shouldn't make yourselves at home among the sexually promiscuous. I didn't mean that you should have nothing at all to do with outsiders of that sort. Or with crooks, whether blue- or white-collar. Or with spiritual phonies, for that matter. You'd have to leave the world entirely to do that!

1 Corinthians 5:9–10

The upshot of this verse is that God has not required you and me to move to the mountains or to join a monastery in order to be a Christian. While we are not of the world, we are still in it; and that means we will have to relate to all kinds of people. It does not take a spiritual giant to know when a thought, word, action—or a friendship—is contrary to the "new life" that is now governing your inner man. However, you can still reach out to those who do not yet know Christ. Scripture testifies of Jesus: "But the Pharisees and the teachers of the law muttered, 'This man welcomes sinners and eats with them'" (Luke 15:2, NIV).

Let's examine this closely. First of all, if Jesus "welcomed" sinners to meals, where did this take place? In his book *Jesus Before Christianity*, Albert Nolan suggests, "It is difficult to understand how Jesus could have been accused of entertaining sinners if he did not have some kind of home in which to do so."[14] Though Scripture does not explicitly tell us that Christ had a home, it is very possible that He did. Apparently, when He was not traveling, Christ would often invite the low end of the social strata to share meals with Him. *Yes, Jesus spent time with* (gasp) *sinners.* He welcomed sinners into His home. In doing so, He displayed the unconditional love that characterizes God. "God is love, and he who abides in love abides in God, and God in him" (1 John 4:16, NKJV).

However, it is important to note that while Jesus befriended sinners in order to witness to them, *He did not invite them into His inner circle.* Hebrews 4:15 says, "This

27

High Priest of ours understands our weaknesses since he had the same temptations we do, though he never once gave way to them and sinned" (TLB). Jesus did not sin with sinners in order to win them, nor did He make them close or intimate friends. That privilege was held exclusively for His disciples, with whom He traveled, ate, slept and lived throughout His ministry. We must follow His lead. Scripture is clear that it is not wise to forge intimate friendships with those who have not embraced Christ as their Savior. The Bible warns:

> Do not be yoked together with unbelievers. For what do righteousness and wickedness have in common? Or what fellowship can light have with darkness? . . . What does a believer have in common with an unbeliever?
>
> 2 Corinthians 6:14–15, NIV

Notice the word *yoked*? Yoking refers to the practice of joining two animals at the neck or head in the same harness for working together, drawing a load or pulling a plow. The whole concept of yoking contains an incredibly important principle reaching back to Old Testament Law. God commanded His people: "You shall not plow with an ox and a donkey together" (Deuteronomy 22:10, NKJV). Unequal yoking was not only an unwise practice; it was also cruel to the animals. The ox is a primarily docile, submitted, easygoing beast. The donkey can be stubborn, resents authority and will eat almost anything. Put the two together and it spells trouble. The donkey will fight the bit and bridle, bite the ox, kick against being led and stop to eat things very damaging to the ox. It is not hard to grasp what Paul was getting at with a Christian and an unbeliever being yoked together.

The above verse (22:10) is sandwiched between two similar commands. In Deuteronomy 22:9 Israel was commanded not to sow their vineyards with different kinds of seeds, "lest the yield of the seed which you have sown and the fruit of your vineyard be defiled" (NKJV). They were also commanded not to wear a garment of different materials, such as wool and linen mixed together. Why? Because pure material is stronger than materials that have been mixed.

A common theme runs throughout these examples: *Weakness is the result of unequal yoking.* When Paul instructed the Corinthian believers not to be unequally yoked with unbelievers, he was not teaching elitism or a "holier than thou" attitude. Paul knew that, like the ox and the donkey, believers and unbelievers possess different natures. Whom you are yoked to matters, because you will go where that person goes, eat what that person eats (spiritually speaking) and experience the inevitable tug-of-war over which god the two of you will serve. The message is clear. Animals of totally different natures should not be yoked together, and the same is true for human beings.

> THE MESSAGE IS CLEAR. ANIMALS OF TOTALLY DIFFERENT NATURES SHOULD NOT BE YOKED TOGETHER, AND THE SAME IS TRUE FOR HUMAN BEINGS.

When God's yoking principle is not honored, the results can be disastrous. Our adversary has no smoother door of entry into our lives than through the emotional ties of an unequal yoking. It has been said that when God wants to bless you, He brings a person into your life. And when Satan wants to destroy you, he brings a person into your life. Many of God's best and brightest have been brought down as a result of the corruption resulting from unequal yoking. Follow me to the next chapter and let's explore the danger of relationships that corrupt.

FRIENDSHIPS THAT CORRUPT

Do not be misled: "Bad company corrupts good character."

1 Corinthians 15:33, NIV

College was a lonely experience for me. I had chosen to live with my parents and commute to the campus for purely selfish reasons—it was free. Attending what was known far and wide as a party school brought immediate isolation because, as already stated, I had made a total commitment to Christ in my late teens; I understood very well the power of friendships to either take you up or pull you down.

As a young teenager, the wrong friends had been instrumental in my walking down a road that was highly destructive; so much so that my conversion to Christ took place in a juvenile detention center where I was being held for involvement with drugs. It was small-time stuff as drug charges go, but big-time to me. Extended jail time grew far too close for comfort. It genuinely scared the ba-jeebies out of me. One of the steps I knew I must take was to sever the friendships that had been so influential in taking me down the wrong path. There is absolutely no way on the planet you can walk with Christ while maintaining friendships with people who do not do the same. Forming new friendships was a crucial part of my journey as a new Christian.

But I also learned early on that to walk away from questionable friendships guaranteed some loneliness. In fact, if you take a strong stand for Christ, you usually do not have to do the walking away—others will do it for you. Jesus said, "If you find the godless world is hating you, remember it got its start hating me" (John 15:18). I certainly was not perfect, but I did take a strong stand for Christ on a campus that was very dark spiritually.

This darkness was made painfully clear in a film class I took as part of my major in radio, television and film. The final assignment at the end of the semester was for each student to produce his or her own short film. It was the student's job to write the script and then serve as the on-camera talent. Audio and lighting persons, camera operators and floor managers were provided from the class. It being just weeks before Christmas, I decided to do a film on the uncanny accuracy of Old Testament Bible prophecy concerning Jesus Christ. *Surely*, I thought, *this will appeal to the intellectual curiosity of my peers.* Oh, sad naïveté. Was I in for a shock!

When the day arrived for my presentation, I was nervous and excited at the same time. I entered class armed with cue cards spelling out verses like Micah 5:2.

"But you, Bethlehem Ephrathah, though you are little among the thousands of Judah, yet out of you shall come forth to Me the one to be Ruler in Israel, whose goings forth are from of old, from everlasting."

NKJV

"This will nail it," I mused. Who could deny the fact that Micah accurately predicted the invasion of planet Earth by a person whose activities spanned eternity and that He was born in Bethlehem! I envisioned being surrounded by curious classmates following my blockbuster film.

Lights, camera, action! Staring into the camera, I reeled off the selected verses and their fulfillment in history. While speaking, I became aware of movement to my right, a sort of continual rustling noise. Not wanting to turn away from the camera, I continued to the end. When the lights came up, the truth of what had happened hit me like a brick on the head. *All my classmates had walked out, including the teacher.* Mind you, my peers were supposed to critique my film, as was the teacher. It was part of the class. The only person left standing in the room was a girl who was also a Christian. "I'm sorry, Jeff," she said, embarrassed for me. You would have thought I had hung upside down from the ceiling lights making monkey noises!

Walking out into the hall, I spotted all my peers leaning against the wall talking, their eyes avoiding me. Passing by them, I felt crushed and humiliated. On the bus ride home, the familiar sights raced by in a meaningless blur. Feeling like the world's biggest fool, my mind sifted through various Bible passages in search of some word of comfort. The words of the apostle Paul floated to the forefront: "Don't become partners with those who reject God. How can you make a partnership out of right and wrong? That's not partnership; that's war" (2 Corinthians 6:14).

War is exactly what had been waged in class that day. My peers were not walking in the light, and something very spiritual had taken place. As I had quoted Scriptures about Christ, the truth of God's Word had made a declaration of war on their lifestyles. Jesus spoke clearly about this: "Everyone who makes a practice of doing evil, addicted to denial and illusion, *hates God-light and won't come near it,* fearing a painful exposure" (John 3:20–21, italics mine).

"Hates God-light." I did not realize walking into class that day that I had carried with me the equivalent of a laser gun, an X-ray machine, a divine exposer of the works of darkness. This is precisely what God's Word says of itself: "His powerful Word is sharp as a surgeon's scalpel, cutting through everything, whether doubt or defense, laying us open to listen and obey" (Hebrews 4:12).

It made no difference that we had shared common interests, were the same age or attended the same school. The response to my film reflected something far deeper at work. A spiritual dynamic was at play. A line of demarcation had been drawn in the sands of our souls. Below the surface, where "deep answers to deep," there existed a difference between us as far apart as the east is from the west and light is from dark.

When you and I take a strong stand for Christ, the only people who can handle it on a consistent basis are those who are in the same boat. Listen carefully to the apostle Paul as he continues his discussion on relationships.

> Is light best friends with dark? Does Christ go strolling with the Devil? Do trust and mistrust hold hands? Who would think of setting up pagan idols in God's holy Temple? But that is exactly what we are, each of us a temple in whom God lives.
>
> 2 Corinthians 6:14–16

When a person who walks with Christ begins to spend time with someone walking in darkness, an inevitable clashing of kingdoms will arise—the Kingdom of heaven with the kingdom of darkness. One or the other will eventually yield. What was initially a very crushing experience for me ultimately became a source of blessing. Following this incident the friendship issue became even clearer for me. Who or what was most important in my life? Did I want the smile of men while incurring the frown of God? Or did I long for the smile of my heavenly Father though the entire world turned and walked away? Every committed follower of Christ must face this question.

The apostle Peter, who was no stranger to persecution, encouraged us: "Be happy when you are insulted for being a Christian, for then the glorious Spirit of God rests upon you" (1 Peter 4:14, NLT).

Another angle to my experience occurred to me on that long bus ride home. What had my classmates been afraid of? According to Scripture, it was "the light of God's truth." They recoiled at being confronted by truth and had no qualms whatsoever separating from me. *Why, then, I thought, was it "holier than thou" snobbery for people walking in the light to seek the same type of separation as those walking in the dark do?* I had often heard criticism of Christians for being "uppity" or "snooty" because they did not run around with those who lived a lifestyle displeasing to Christ. They certainly had no problem at all taking their stand and separating from me. Why, then, should I run around with them? The answer is that I should not, and neither should you.

Just because you may get along well with someone, have good chemistry or experience mutual attraction does not mean a friendship is being ordered by God. In cases where emotions are involved, I have learned, sometimes the hard way, to always follow the principles of Scripture, not fickle feelings. "He who trusts in himself is a fool, but he who walks in wisdom is kept safe" (Proverbs 28:26, NIV).

Following this painful event, one of the guys in my class with whom I had gotten along well (we never did discuss the exodus from class) began to befriend me. *Wow!* I thought. *At least I'm not a pariah to him!* It was like fresh air to have someone actually seem interested in getting to know me. It is the lonely and blue times that place us in the greatest danger of hooking up with the wrong kinds of friends. "He who is full loathes honey, but to the hungry even what is bitter tastes sweet" (Proverbs 27:7, NIV). When our needs are shouting for attention, discernment takes a backseat. Crying needs can muffle a protesting conscience.

"Bill" and I began to hang together, talking between classes, shooting a little bit of pool—all innocent stuff. One day he invited me to stay over for the night. By now I had a car that released me from having to take the bus, so I agreed to stay. After piddling around with some homework, it was time to hit the hay. It was a small apartment, so I was elected to sleep on the floor. After Bill had gone to his room, I lay down and turned over sideways at just the right angle for my eyes to fall on a huge stack of pornographic magazines. This was not what I needed to see. I was single, and like most Christian guys I knew, fought hard to walk in moral purity.

The first impulse to wash over me said, "No one would ever know. Just take a quick look." *Maybe I could look at a cover or two without opening them,* I thought. But who was I kidding? With the pull becoming stronger by the moment, I knew that if I stayed, I would look. A battle with conflicting thoughts raged within. *You're being too religious. Chill! After all, Bill is just a normal guy, right? Why not be more like him? Live a little!* At that moment I realized that I could not bring into my inner circle of close or best friends anyone who had not chosen to be a totally dedicated disciple of Christ, no matter how lonely I felt. To do so would be to learn their ways and lose the cutting edge of my walk with God. Knocking on his door, I told Bill that I was not feeling well and hit the road.

IT IS THE LONELY AND BLUE TIMES THAT PLACE US IN THE GREATEST DANGER OF HOOKING UP WITH THE WRONG KINDS OF FRIENDS.

My leaving was not an indictment of Bill. He simply did not know Christ like I did. I did what I had to do to remain true to my faith. Just because we got along well was no justification for forming a close friendship, nor was it a sign that God was in it. For instance, the Bible says that Herod and Pilate became fast friends while both playing their part in crucifying Jesus. Talk about a friendship made in hell!

Then Herod and his soldiers were very bad to Jesus and made fun of Him. They put a beautiful coat on Him and sent Him back to Pilate. That day Pilate and Herod became friends. Before that they had worked against each other.

Luke 23:11–12, NLV

Listen closely to Paul as he continues his exhortation to the Corinthian church on the topic of friendships:

God himself put it this way: "I'll live in them, move into them; I'll be their God and they'll be my people. So leave the corruption and compromise; leave it for good," says God. "Don't link up with those who will pollute you. I want you all for myself. I'll be a Father to you; you'll be sons and daughters to me."

2 Corinthians 6:16–18

The Bible warns that when the children of light link up with those walking in darkness, compromise followed by corruption will result. Paul wrote in another place, "Do not be so deceived and misled! Evil companionships (communion, associations) corrupt and deprave good manners and morals and character" (1 Corinthians 15:33, AMPLIFIED).

Caught by Corruption

If good manners, morals and character can be torpedoed by something called corruption, then we should understand what "corrupt" means. "Corrupt" comes from a Greek word meaning "to pine or waste; to shrivel or wither; to spoil or ruin; to wane; to destroy, to bring into a worse state morally and spiritually."[1] Corruption takes place in pale shades of gray, not clear blacks and whites. It is stealthy, progressing slowly but surely like an unseen cancer of the soul.

While *corrupt* is the word Paul selects to describe the dire effects of ungodly company, he also uses it to describe the old sinful nature from which Christians have been de-

37

livered. "You were taught, with regard to your former way of life, to put off your old self, which is being *corrupted* by its deceitful desires" (Ephesians 4:22, NIV, italics mine).

Picture for a moment a beautiful apple tree, healthy and flourishing. It is filled with bright, luscious, red apples. Now imagine the beautiful green leaves first turning brown, then withering and finally falling off. Next, the once bright-red apples become shrunken and infested with worms. It has not happened overnight, but incrementally, over time; almost imperceptibly to the casual observer the insidious process of rot and decay has taken its toll. This is a picture of corruption. Corruption is the gradual process by which godly character withers, spiritual health fades and strong morals drop away like rotted fruit from a once-healthy spiritual life.

> CORRUPTION TAKES PLACE IN PALE SHADES OF GRAY, NOT CLEAR BLACKS AND WHITES. IT IS STEALTHY, PROGRESSING SLOWLY BUT SURELY LIKE AN UNSEEN CANCER OF THE SOUL.

As I already pointed out, "corrupt" is found in the New Testament often. In his second letter to the Corinthian church, Paul again declares, "We have *corrupted* no man" (7:2, KJV, italics mine). In warning his fellow believers about false teachers, Jude wrote, "But these speak evil of whatever they do not know; and whatever they know naturally, like brute beasts, in these things they corrupt themselves" (Jude 10, NKJV).

Based on what we now know about wrong friendships, 1 Corinthians 15:33 could read as follows (let's call this the revised Wickwire version): "Don't be fooled and led down the wrong path! Associating with the wrong people will cause your spiritual life to waste, shrivel and wither; and the fruit of your once-healthy walk with God will become worm-eaten and die."

Unfortunately, the last person to recognize the process of corruption taking place is the one being corrupted. That is what makes corruption so deadly. C. S. Lewis wrote, "The safest road to hell is the gradual one—the gentle slope, soft underfoot, without sudden turnings, without milestones, without signposts."[2]

Israel: The Wrong and Blinding Road

One of the clearest examples of corruption through wrong relationships is found in Psalm 106. In this anonymous psalm of confession for the sins of Israel, five *stages of corruption* are detailed.

First, Israel "mingled" with God's enemies. "They did not destroy the peoples, concerning whom the LORD had commanded them, but they *mingled* with the Gentiles" (Psalm 106:34–35, NKJV, italics mine). Though it seems severe and cruel to the modern mind that God would command His people to utterly destroy the ungodly nations that were occupying the Promised Land, it was "undoubtedly based upon God's foreknowledge that . . . there would be contact, and if contact, then contamination."[3]

> CORRUPTION IS THE GRADUAL PROCESS BY WHICH GODLY CHARACTER WITHERS, SPIRITUAL HEALTH FADES AND STRONG MORALS DROP AWAY LIKE ROTTED FRUIT FROM A ONCE-HEALTHY SPIRITUAL LIFE.

The word *mingled* means "to braid," as one might braid hair by wrapping three strands around each other; a strong picture of the emotional intertwining involved in relationships.[4] It also means "to have fellowship with," or "to share in something." Instead of practicing the total separation God had required of them, Israel befriended and fellowshiped with people whose lifestyles were an abomination to the Lord. Perhaps they

39

thought: *We can handle it. Our faith is strong. We don't want to appear stuck-up or unfriendly.* But they did not handle it and came to the brink of ruin.

Next, a chilling picture is painted of that "gentle slope" downward that C. S. Lewis so aptly described. The New Life Version of Scripture says, "But they mixed with the nations and *learned* their ways" (Psalm 106:35, italics mine). *The Message* is even more descriptive: ". . . and in time became just like them." Thinking they could dance around the edge of the flame, God's own chosen people began to look like, talk like, think like and live just like the people whose ways God despised! The heathen did not become more like God's people; God's people became more like them.

But the process did not stop there. It never does. Next, Israel became practicing idolaters. "They *served* their idols, which became a snare to them" (Psalm 106:36, NKJV, italics mine). Think of it. The people who had personally witnessed almighty God sending plague after plague upon their cruel taskmasters in order to deliver them from Egypt; who were eye-witnesses of God's power splitting the Red Sea, dividing it into two glistening walls of water for them to safely cross over; who followed the supernatural cloud by day and fire by night; these same people descended into serving dumb, lifeless, wooden idols that could not speak, hear or see!

> A WRONG RELATIONSHIP IS THE ENEMY'S SMOOTHEST POINT OF ENTRY INTO THE LIFE OF THE GODLY.

The Bible reveals that once they reached this level of stunning servitude, they became "snared." "Snare" is translated from a Hebrew word meaning "a noose for catching animals," or "a hook for the nose."[5] God's chosen people, who ignored His warnings, were now trapped like an animal hung by a rope, or like a fish hooked in the snout. This is precisely what the enemy is after in his endless attempts to trap believers today. He seeks to corrupt our walk and ruin our testimony. The tempter knows that we will learn the ways of those we befriend, and their vices and downfalls will also become ours. As already stated, a wrong relationship is the enemy's smoothest point of entry into the life of the godly.

What follows next is hard to believe. God's people now descended into the very pit of depravity. "They even sacrificed their sons and their daughters to demons, and shed innocent blood, the blood of their sons and daughters, whom they sacrificed to the idols of Canaan; and the land was polluted with blood" (Psalm 106:37–38, NKJV).

Do you believe for one moment that when the children of Israel began to associate with the ungodly, they could have imagined in the furthest reaches of their minds that they would one day place their precious children on an altar of fire to gain the favor of false gods; or that they would personally worship demons or sacrifice their flesh-and-blood offspring to evil spirits? But they did! This is the chilling power of corruption.

Corruption through wrong relationships does not take place overnight; rather, it occurs over time in a thousand decisions and missteps, each one carrying its victim farther down the slippery slope toward destruction. Corruption feeds on minor compromises, seemingly insignificant surrenders that, when added together, comprise a great fall. Let's recall the steps Israel took on their way down:

> *Mingled* (they fellowshiped with the ungodly), which led to
>
> *Learned* (they learned and practiced ungodly ways), which led to
>
> *Served* (they became subservient to false gods), which led to

Ensnarement (they experienced bondage, entrapment to false gods), which led to

Sacrifice (they gave up something of great value to a god, which is the essence of worship)

How the Mighty Have Fallen

Another striking example of how corruption happens through wrong relationships is that of wise old King Solomon. Although his downfall came through ill-advised marriages to foreign women, the principle of corruption via relationships still holds true. When Solomon was young and still under the influence of his father, David, his heart was clearly in pursuit of God. "And Solomon loved the LORD, walking in the statutes of his father David" (1 Kings 3:3, NKJV). When he was appointed king, the young ruler's only request to God was for wisdom in order that he might lead God's people successfully (see 1 Kings 3:5–14). Yet stunningly, Solomon's life was almost completely destroyed by corruption. The Bible clearly describes what happened:

> But King Solomon loved many foreign women . . . women of the Moabites, Ammonites, Edomites, Sidonians, and Hittites—from the nations of whom the LORD had said to the children of Israel, "You shall not intermarry with them, nor they with you. Surely they will turn away your hearts after their gods." Solomon clung to these in love.
>
> 1 Kings 11:1–2, NKJV

God knew that if His people mixed with idolaters, corruption would result. This is precisely what happened to the richest and wisest man on earth, whose fame had spread throughout the known world; the same man who had humbly prayed for wisdom. The Bible describes the tragic facts:

"For it was so, when Solomon was old, that his wives turned his heart after other gods; and his heart was not loyal to the LORD his God" (verse 4, NKJV).

The gods that the wayward King Solomon succumbed to on his downward path of corruption are mind-numbing. "For Solomon went after Ashtoreth the goddess of the Sidonians, and after Milcom the abomination of the Ammonites" (verse 5, NKJV). Milcom (Molech) was the fire-god of the Ammonites. The sacrifices offered to him were those of children who were made to pass through the fire to their death.

But Solomon's idolatry did not stop there. Remember, because corruption is incremental, it can lead one to a destination that is simply unimaginable from the vantage point of where one first began.

> Then Solomon built a high place for Chemosh the abomi-nation of Moab . . . and for Molech the abomination of the people of Ammon. And he did likewise for all his foreign wives, who burned incense and sacrificed to their gods.
>
> 1 Kings 11:7–8, NKJV

The king, whose high and lofty calling had included building a splendid temple for the worship of the true and living God, now turned his brilliance and talents toward building abominable places of worship for idols, which was tantamount to placing his kingly approval on them. This was a dark and tragic hour in Israel's history. How could a man with such a high calling, spiritual knowledge and godly upbringing come to this? *Corruption through wrong relationships.*

The gods of Solomon's companions became his gods. He began to worship what they worshiped. He learned their ways, and their ways became a snare to his soul. God had graciously given to Solomon unparalleled wisdom, wealth and power, which all were turned against the Creator. Sadly, these were his last works, done in his old age rather than his youth. "The light which God had kindled did not flame out into eternal glory, but went out in eternal night."[6] The king with a divided heart left a divided kingdom that split and spiraled downward following his death.

While corruption is very stealthy and gradual, there are signposts along the way. The following are some warning flags to look for. If any of these register with you or someone you know, my sincere prayer is that God will help you to turn to Him with all your heart and reverse the process of corruption so that you may once again walk in the light. You can know you are in a corrupting relationship if:

- You must compromise long-held biblical, moral and ethical convictions to remain in it.
- Your relationship with God is not what it was before the friendship.
- You are involved in activities that at first brought great conviction, but conviction's voice is now but a fading whisper.
- There is a nagging sense deep down that, no matter how hard you try to justify it, something is wrong in your relationship.
- People who love you are warning you about your relationship.

If even one of these warning flags is true, you should reassess your relationship and make whatever decisions are necessary to bring yourself fully into the light. You may need to seek the assistance of a Christian counselor or church leadership to end the relationship. And you will need to surround yourself with praying friends who can stand with you. Whatever it takes, become proactive by separating yourself from friendships that corrupt. "Make level paths for your feet and take only ways that are firm" (Proverbs 4:26, NIV).

If corrupting relationships are a fact of life, life-giving friendships are, as well. In fact, God brings friends our way, not only for our enjoyment, but also for His purposes. What does a godly friend look like? How can we know that a friendship has the smile of heaven upon it? Let's explore this question in the next chapter.

3

WHAT A GODLY FRIEND
LOOKS LIKE

He allowed him to go to see his friends
so they could care for him.

Acts 27:3, WE

My wife, Cathy, just received a birthday card from an old friend hearkening back to her childhood. Gaye walked into her place of employment out of the blue and handed it to her in person, a big smile stretching across her face. On the front is a picture of two young girls—around seven years old—in bathing suits. They are running through a sprinkler in someone's yard while holding a little umbrella and laughing with all their might, eyes squinting to dodge the spray. It is a snapshot of friendship begun early, of friendship's beautiful innocence. On the inside, the card says:

*Cathy—when I saw this card I thought of us!
Remember playing in the water with the Mr.*

Wiggles thing? I do! Hope you have a great
birthday!
Love,
Gaye

After reading it again at home, Cathy teared up. I knew
what she was thinking but asked anyway. "What's the matter?" I said, while hitting the mute button on the TV to give
her my full attention.

"Oh, you know, so many friendships just seem to fade away
or go bad. But after all these years—marriages, kids and
really going our separate ways—this one is still there. It just
means so much that someone I knew before 'life' happened
is still around, that we still have that connection. I just wish
they could all be this way," she said with a slight sigh.

I understood. It is rare indeed to still enjoy a friendship
that reaches back to early childhood, someone who has
known you basically forever. Cathy, however, has been for-
tunate enough to have two of them. Cheryl, whose friendship also stretched back to childhood, just recently died
following a valiant fight against cancer. While she was sick,
Cathy would hop a plane and fly to Oklahoma for a few
days to care for her as often as possible.

Those were bittersweet visits, but still smacked of the
deep friendship they had enjoyed. One time Cathy visited
during her birthday. Though Cheryl's health had fast been
waning, she remembered her friend's special day and instructed her daughter to get a candle, stick it in a chocolate-
covered donut, light it and walk in singing "Happy Birthday." Even at death's door she remembered the date and
that Cathy loves chocolate.

Toward the end, her lifelong friend could not get out of
bed. To shine a little levity on the situation, they would sit
for hours rehashing memories that cancer could not steal.
They laughed. They cried. Life can be so unfair sometimes,
so heartless. This was surely one of those times.

When Cathy last hugged her, she sensed the end was probably near. It was not too long afterward that she got the call she had so dreaded. Her memory of Cheryl's funeral is a blur seen through tears and more tears. Somehow, at Cheryl's request, Cathy delivered the eulogy. It was surreal, as death so often is. *How could my lifelong friend no longer be on the other end of a phone call, or waiting at the airport, or in a new letter in the mailbox?* she thought. But friendships like these leave tracks on our soul, imprints that remain long after death has taken the person away. Through the years, Cheryl had played a part in who Cathy became and is inextricably wound up in the tapestry of her soul. No wonder the proverb says, "The memory of the righteous is blessed" (Proverbs 10:7, NKJV).

This all made Gaye's surprise visit so much more meaningful. Cathy remarked that, though it had been around a year since they had last seen each other, when she walked in it was as if she had never been gone. Best friends are that way. It is these kinds of friendships that provide a distant echo of what it must have been like before the Fall, before we became so broken; they are the exception rather than the rule. "Every spark of beauty, worth and meaning that we experience in this strange existence glimmers as a relic of a good world that still bears the mark of its original design," observes Philip Yancey.[1]

I believe there is a longing deep inside each of us for the way things were meant to be before the tragedy of sin crippled our world. This is why there is so much disappointment, sort of an ongoing letdown, with relationships of all kinds. It might be compared to what I have read about some amnesiacs who, though they experience a slight recognition of people and surroundings, do not know why. They are lost in an erased memory yet long to recapture their original identity. Deep inside of us lies the concept, the divine stamp of what God intended for friendships. We believe, against all evidence otherwise, in love and permanence and the unbroken chain of affection, and are deeply disappointed when that belief is shattered by the inability to experience it. It is this longing that lay behind Cathy's quiet sigh.

For those of us who have embraced Christ—the last Adam—the disappointment is doubled when friendships go awry. While the first Adam brought sin on the entire human race, the last Adam, Christ Jesus, came to undo all of that, to restore what was broken. "Death initially came by a man, and resurrection from death came by a man. Everybody dies in Adam; everybody comes alive in Christ" (1 Corinthians 15:21–22). Based on this fact, Christians expect to see the light of His restoration breaking through into their relationships, and when it does not happen, the double whammy of deferred hope takes the wind out of our faith.

Let's face it, when Christ comes into a person's life, a whole set of expectations comes with Him. Because He so dramatically changes us, we project that same expectation onto other areas, relationships being at the top of the list. For instance, when we enter our first church, we expect the people there to be unlike the ones we have known in the world. We anticipate finding love, acceptance, graciousness and mercy. When we encounter otherwise, it can greatly sour our experience, even causing us to stumble in our faith. "How is the Christ we see in Scripture," we ask, "not manifesting Himself in those who say they know Him? Especially in church, which is His house?"

I will never forget a sharp-looking, successful African American man who came to see me one day. As he sat in my office and began to share what was on his heart, anger rolled up into his face, and disillusionment with Christianity began spilling out in his words. He had offered to serve in a well-known church in town for what had by now amounted to years, not for money, but just to reach out to people. Over and over again he had been put off and offered flimsy excuses, and he was finally encouraged to open up a mission work downtown, miles from the church. "I know," he said with anger and hurt shooting from his eyes, "that the issue is the color of my skin. Prejudice is alive and well in the Church. I thought God was love! What do I do with what I've experienced?"

I told him I would rather go where I am celebrated, not tolerated, and that he should find another place to worship. I then did my best to explain that this conduct did not reflect the heart of Christ, and that the actions of those church members could only be relegated to immaturity and carnality. I never saw him again and truly pray that he discovered a more mature body of believers that embraces all people alike.

I share this story as just another example of how failed expectations happen in relationships where the Christ we see in Scripture is not the Christ we encounter in others. Yet, we never stop hoping. Though just as many Christians as non-Christians divorce,[2] our belief in love, romance and lifelong commitment still drives us to the altar believing we will somehow be different. While so many have experienced disappointment, we still hold out a trembling hand of friendship in hopes that this time it will change.

One reason I believe the Bible to be the Word of God is its stark honesty about the lives of its heroes. We are told the truth about Abraham's fearful lie about Sarah being his half sister rather than his wife, David's adultery, Samson's womanizing, Peter's denial of Christ and Paul's disappointment with some of his friendships. I, for one, am thankful that the great apostle to the Gentiles told the truth about his relational letdowns. It encourages me to see that, even though Paul was burned by friendship, he kept reaching out for the real thing. Here are just a few examples of his honest confessions. It might help you to know that all of the following quotes are taken from his second letter to Timothy, just prior to what he knew to be his impending martyrdom. At the end of his life, the sting of friendships that failed was still fresh on his mind. "At my preliminary hearing no one stood by me. They all ran like scared rabbits" (2 Timothy 4:16). The long line of people in Asia Paul had led to Christ, loved and befriended left him alone and without support as he was brought before Caesar for his testimony of Christ.

"For Demas, because he loved this world, has deserted me" (2 Timothy 4:10, NIV). In Colossians we find Demas greeting the church as Paul's fellow laborer, only to find later that he deserted him.

"This you know, that all those in Asia have turned away from me, among whom are Phygellus and Hermogenes" (2 Timothy 1:15, NIV). Paul was a name-dropper. If his experience with you was good, he named you. If bad, he named you. I can hear the same sigh in his voice that I heard in Cathy's that night. It is the sigh that says, "This is not what it was meant to be."

Let me be honest about something. If I were going to go on vacation with one of the apostles, Paul would not be my first choice. Instead, I would likely choose Peter or John for the simple reason that I think Peter would have been a blast and John easygoing. I just cannot imagine saying to Paul, "Hey, Paul, let's hit the pool!" Or, "Paul, let's rent some bikes, ride to the beach, grab a boat and try parasailing!" Somehow, I just cannot envision the great apostle to the Gentiles standing on the end of a boat waiting to be yanked off the deck into the wild blue. But Peter? Oh yeah. He would probably want to try it without the sail. And it is not hard to picture John in a colorful Hawaiian shirt, kicked back in a hammock.

Whether or not he was difficult to get along with, Paul also enjoyed many friends, who were fiercely loyal to him. His perseverance in friendship paid off. He shows us that Christ can indeed restore some of what God intended for friendships before we were broken. They remind me of that great friendship verse found in Proverbs: "A friend loves at all times. He is there to help when trouble comes" (17:17, NIrv). Paul closed out his letter to the Colossian church with a roll call of six faithful friends, naming each of them. Fortunately for us, he identified each one's unique characteristics, painting a beautiful picture of what a godly friend looks like. Let's take a look at the friendship traits that stuck out in Paul's mind.

Tychicus: Fitting into God's Plan

Tychicus possessed a servant's heart. He fit beautifully into God's purpose for Paul, and Paul fit into his. Tychicus (pronounced "tik'-ik-us") is mentioned five times in the New Testament. His name means "fortuitous."[3] Several words come to mind every time Paul mentions his friend: *faithful, dependable, trustworthy, good friend, trusted minister, trusted companion.* "Tychicus, my good friend here, will tell you what I'm doing and how things are going with me. He is certainly a dependable servant of the Master!" (Ephesians 6:21).

You can almost hear relief in Paul's voice as he touts his friend's character. And little wonder, for this is the same apostle who knew the pain of abandonment all too well: "Demas has deserted me" (2 Timothy 4:10, NLT). "The first time I was brought before the judge, no one came with me. Everyone abandoned me" (2 Timothy 4:16, NLT).

But with Tychicus the old apostle had struck friendship gold. When the heat was on, Tychicus stuck like glue. When Paul needed something done, Tychicus was humbly willing to serve his friend in the ministry. Servanthood was his crowning characteristic. Each time he is mentioned it involves Paul sending him somewhere with a message. Tychicus was Paul's Western Union man. "Tychicus . . . will tell you all the news about me. I am sending him to you for this very purpose, that he may know your circumstances and comfort your hearts" (Colossians 4:7–8, NKJV).

Tychicus modeled the principle that friendship is not a "What can you do for me?" proposition, a guaranteed friendship buster. Tychicus was not hanging with Paul looking to spruce up his résumé. He became part of Paul's success by comforting and encouraging the churches with the news that their apostle was experiencing joy and victory, even in his imprisonment. The approaching figure of Tychicus lifted their hearts because he was always the bearer of good news and ever the encourager. "Anxiety in a man's heart weighs it down, but a good word makes it glad" (Proverbs 12:25, NASB).

One valuable lesson we can learn from Paul's friendship with Tychicus is that a godly friendship will fit into and enhance God's purpose for your life. The child of God should never tolerate a friendship that cannot fit into God's plan. Never give room to a close or intimate friendship that cannot make room for your highest calling. You should be free to talk about the Lord, go to meetings and pray together with your friends. Any friend worth having will fit into and complement God's plan for your life, and you into theirs.

Tychicus possessed a servant's heart and fit beautifully into God's purpose for Paul.

Onesimus: A Model of Obedience under Pressure

Onesimus was once a runaway slave. His gripping testimony of hopeless desperation turned to joy would have made him a hot ticket on today's speaking circuit. You can read about him in the brief letter to Philemon, neatly tucked in between Titus and Hebrews. Of him, Paul would proudly write, "Onesimus is one of you, and has become such a trusted and dear brother!" (Colossians 4:9). Onesimus, whose name means "useful, profitable," was a native of Colossae, home of the Colossian church, which is likely why Paul told the Colossians that he was "one of your number" (Colossians 4:9, NASB).[4]

Onesimus's story begins one day when he had had enough of the misery of slavery and decided to cut and run. During his escape from the household of his master, Philemon, he apparently robbed him. Paul hints at this when he later writes to Philemon, "If he has wronged you or owes anything, put that on my account" (Philemon 18, NKJV). Onesimus fled to Rome, where he hoped to disappear for good. But God had other plans. As he wandered the busy streets, he encountered the great apostle Paul. *Of all the people to run into!* he must have thought. Even back then the world was a very small, connected place—especially if God was hot on your trail.

Speaking of small worlds, not only was Paul the king of preachers at the time, he also had led Philemon to Christ. And the Colossian church had been meeting in his house! The great apostle led the shaken and frightened runaway to Christ. "While here in jail," Paul later wrote to Philemon, "I've fathered a child, so to speak. And here he is, hand-carrying this letter—Onesimus!" (Philemon 10). From runaway slave to "trusted and dear brother," Onesimus became a positive addition to Paul's ministry and life. To Philemon he again writes, "who once was unprofitable to you, but now is profitable to you and to me" (Philemon 11, NKJV).

The friendship characteristic that stands out most with Onesimus is that of *humbling himself to obey the will of God, no matter the cost.* You see, Paul had asked Onesimus to return home to Philemon. Talk about facing your past to make things right! Lest this particular aspect of the story be misunderstood, let me be clear. Paul was not placing his stamp of approval on slavery. The apostle wrote in Galatians, "There is neither . . . slave nor free . . . in Christ Jesus" (3:28, NKJV). And in his letter to Philemon he implored, "that you might receive him forever, no longer as a slave but more than a slave—a beloved brother" (Philemon 15–16, NKJV). Paul was sending Onesimus back for the sake of restoration.

It was a long journey from Rome back to Colossae. The former runaway slave had plenty of opportunity to change his mind and run again, but he did not. He was willing to humble himself before God in order to set things right.

Onesimus displayed the friendship traits of humility and obedience to God, no matter what the cost.

Think about your own friends for a moment. Have you observed in them a willingness to pay a personal price of discomfort, loss or inconvenience in order to obey God? Would your present friends humble themselves to ask forgiveness, go a second mile, walk away from a strong desire or suffer in any other way in order to pull into line with God's will? If so, that is *huge* in terms of friends worth having.

The ability to break and bow before God reveals a friend who will also be able to say "I'm sorry" when needed. *A godly friend will show the capacity to humble himself or herself in order to get in line with God's will.* He or she will obey the Lord even if it hurts him or her. Onesimus did just that, and Paul called him his friend.

Aristarchus: A Friend in Tough Times

Aristarchus would get in the mud with you—even if it was not *his* mud. We find him in jail with Paul, and he seems very cheery nonetheless! "Aristarchus, who is in jail here with me, sends greetings" (Colossians 4:10). Aristarchus, meaning "the best ruler,"[5] was another of Paul's true friends. Trouble followed Paul everywhere he went. To accompany him was a virtual guarantee of encountering danger, persecution and hardship. Even so, Scripture records that Aristarchus was often there for Paul, sticking like glue in tough times.

Aristarchus hitched his wagon to the controversial apostle on Paul's third missionary journey. Their travels took them to Ephesus, where, along with Paul, Aristarchus was seized and dragged through the city by an angry mob of silversmiths led by a man named Demetrius (see Acts 19:29). From Ephesus they traveled to Greece, then Asia, and finally they were sent together as prisoners to Rome. Tradition says that Aristarchus was finally martyred.

The world is full of fair-weather friends. There for the party and laughs, they always answer the phone when the sun of success is shining and their own needs are being met. But let the bottom drop out, and fair-weather friends soon go foul. When the thrill is gone and the bills come due, they have a genius for disappearing. It is a very sobering experience indeed to reach out for a helping hand from among those who gladly took from you when times were good, only to discover that they have moved on to the next party. The realization that they were not who you thought they were is like a stiff punch in the gut. Scripture observes that "wealth brings many friends, but a poor man's friend deserts him. . . . Though he pursues them with pleading, they are nowhere to be found" (Proverbs 19:4, 7, NIV).

Thankfully, this is not true of the Aristarchuses of life. Aristarchus was at Paul's side when a major storm brought shipwreck to him and all aboard, followed by an unplanned stay on the island of Malta (see Acts 27). Paul referred to him as a "fellow prisoner" to the Colossian believers (Colossians 4:10, NIV). That phrase employs a Greek word that means "prisoner of war." To Paul, Aristarchus was a fellow-soldier in the epic battle between the forces of good and evil. Through all the hardships, he never went AWOL, waved the white flag or walked away from his friend.

The story is told of a group of friends who went deer hunting and paired off in twos for the day. That night one of the hunters returned alone, staggering under an eight-point buck.

"Where's Harry?" he was asked.

"Harry had a stroke of some kind. He's a couple of miles back up the trail."

"You left Harry lying there and carried the deer back?"

"Well," said the hunter, "I figured no one was going to steal Harry."

This story puts a smile on my face; but I have to tell you, I have seen more than a few people leave a needy brother or sister to chase after an "eight-point buck." Paul told the truth about humanity when he said, "For everyone looks out for his own interests, not those of Jesus Christ" (Philippians 2:21, NIV). Unless you come to Christ, humble yourself before Him and die to self, you will live a selfish life as surely as the sun rises in the morning (see Luke 9:23).

Aristarchus' friendship trait was that of faithfulness in trying times.

Have you been through some gut-wrenching, even life-threatening times lately that have thrown you to the mat? Look around you. Which friends stayed true? Who answered the phone at two in the morning when you could not sleep? Who checked on you when they did not have to? Aristarchus would have been there. I concur with Cicero, who said, "Man's best support is a very dear friend."[6]

Justus: A Friend Who Comforts

The significance of Paul's friend Justus is better understood by the paraphrase offered in *The Message*: "and also Jesus, the one they call Justus. These are the only ones left from the old crowd who have stuck with me in working for God's kingdom" (Colossians 4:11).

"The only ones left . . . who have stuck with me." Paul had experienced a large number of helpers falling by the wayside in his efforts to preach the Gospel. It is a deflating experience when formerly exuberant helpers walk away from an effort your heart is invested in. To go from many to few, listening to all the well-constructed excuses, watching familiar faces fade away, is guaranteed to breed faith-crushing discouragement. Only three of Paul's Jewish kinsmen remained. One of them was Justus. Justus walked in when just about everyone else walked out. That is what a godly friend does. A godly friend shares your vision, grabs the plow with you and says, "We're in this together."

In 1987, a Special Olympics track meet was held in Marin County, California. This was the big one for which they had all trained. As the magic moment drew near, nine excited runners crouched, dug their cleats into the track and anxiously waited for the pistol to fire. The stands were packed with excited parents and friends. Video cameras were rolling, cameras were flashing and signs waved back and forth, all cheering their guys on.

From Justus we learn the friendship principle of loyalty, regardless of what others think or do.

Bang! The gun cracked, and the eager nine exploded from the starting line. Hope etched itself across every straining face. Visions of the coveted medals danced in their heads. Then, without warning, the smallest and fastest among them tripped and fell facedown on the track. A pitiful cry of frustration and pain split the air as his dream vanished in an agonizing microsecond.

But here the story takes an incredible turn. His eight peers had heard the anguished scream and knew he was down. Unable to focus on the race, they kept turning and looking back at their buddy lying on the track. Slowly, one of them dropped back and began walking toward his friend. This inspired a chain reaction. Soon they all stopped, turned around and walked resolutely toward their fallen comrade.

The fallen runner lay crumpled and crying. The first one to reach him held out his hand and picked him up. Soon the rest gathered around. In front of a stunned crowd of hushed onlookers, they all joined hands in an unforgettable show of support. As they walked arm in arm toward the finish line, the crowd erupted in cheers and tears.

That remarkable scene was one of those Kodak moments when a powerful truth leaps from an event and brands itself onto your memory. A friend was more important than a medal. Relationship was more valuable than competition and winning. In losing, they had all won. By placing each other above themselves, they had modeled a friendship principle displayed long ago by a disciple of Christ named Justus. "The only ones left . . . who have stuck with me. . . ." And Justus was only a reflection of Jesus Christ, who left everything that He had in order to reach down and pick us up from where we all had fallen on the track of life.

Epaphras: A Friend Who Prays

A praying friend is more valuable than gold. The outstanding friendship characteristic of Epaphras was his powerful intercessory prayer life. "Epaphras, who is one of you, says hello. What a trooper he has been! He's been tireless in his prayers for you, praying that you'll stand firm, mature and confident in everything God wants you to do" (Colossians 4:12).

Epaphras models the value of a praying friend.

Paul called Epaphras (ep' a-fras) his "beloved fellow bond-servant" and "a bond-slave of Jesus Christ." Likely the first pastor of the Colossian church, Epaphras, according to the martyrologies (records of martyrs), suffered martyrdom in Colossae, where he pastored.

While delivering a message one Sunday morning, I said something totally unplanned. "If you have a praying friend, pray they don't die!" Though spoken tongue-in-cheek, the words sprang from a deep well of personal experience. I have been privileged to have some praying friends who prayed me out of some very deep pits. Have you ever felt like you could literally *feel* someone's prayers? If you believe the testimony of Scripture, you surely have a deep conviction about the value of praying friends.

When Paul used the phrase "always laboring fervently for you in prayers" (Colossians 4:12, NKJV), he chose a Greek word for labor that means, "to fight, to engage in a struggle, often an athletic contest."[7] Epaphras had literally stepped into the ring with the devil, wrestling with him over the people under his pastoral care. Do you have friends who pray for you?

Nympha: A Hospitable Friend

Nympha was a prominent Christian woman in Laodicea, whose house was used as a place of worship. Paul singles her out and says, "Give my greetings to the brothers at Laodicea, and to Nympha and the church in her house" (Colossians 4:15, NIV). Very little is known of this godly first-century woman. She is only mentioned once. Yet what we are told reveals much about her, and it is her hospitality that jumps out more than any single thing.

Hospitality is found in the New Testament five times. It means, "the love of strangers."[8] In Romans, Paul commands the saints to be "given to hospitality" (12:13, NKJV), and the elders of the church are commanded to practice hospitality in both 1 Timothy and Titus. The apostle Peter echoed the same theme when he commanded Christians everywhere to "offer hospitality to one another without grumbling" (1 Peter 4:9, NIV). While this principle applies to all people, it also targets the poor. *The Message* puts it this way: "Be quick to give a meal to the hungry, a bed to the homeless—cheerfully."

It has been my privilege for many years now to serve as a senior pastor in three different churches. My wife and I founded each of the three churches, with God's amazing grace ever our indispensable help. Through the years, I have learned something very important; and, in all honesty, what I am about to tell you was not my view of things when I first entered the ministry. I believed that good preaching and strong worship were all that was necessary to attract people to a church. I thought that everything else could be less than stellar and the ship would still sail. I was wrong. I have since learned that the life or death of a church is found in the foyer where people are greeted . . . or not.

> THE LIFE OR DEATH OF A CHURCH IS FOUND IN THE FOYER WHERE PEOPLE ARE GREETED . . . OR NOT.

I can almost feel the hackles rising among some of you reading this book, who are men and women of the Word. You believe that everything begins and ends with solid preaching and teaching. Please do not misunderstand my point. I, too, am a man of Scripture. I have given my life to minister God's Word and have done so since the ripe old age of eighteen. Faith comes by hearing God's Word, and the Christian path is daily illuminated by its awesome light. But hear me on this one: *Never underestimate the power of hospitality and friendship in a church.*

Some churches have the greatest preaching on the planet, but you could ice skate to your seat, they are so cold and unfriendly. Yet there are other churches where the preaching is nominal and the singing frightful, but hospitality oozes out of every square foot—and it is full! People come where they are celebrated, not tolerated. And if that is true for churches, it is also true of friendships. In fact, the Bible says, "A man who has friends must himself be friendly" (Proverbs 18:24, NKJV).

There is a reason that Paul instructed elders of churches to practice hospitality. Hospitality is a reflection of God, who has *received* us because of His Son, Jesus Christ.

> Having predestined us to adoption as sons by Jesus Christ to Himself, according to the good pleasure of His will, to the praise of the glory of His grace, by which He made us accepted in the Beloved.
>
> Ephesians 1:5–6, NKJV

The "Beloved" at the end of the verse is Jesus. We are the "accepted" ones. Because of the sacrifice of Christ on the cross, God has favored us with His grace and accepted us into His family. Through Christ Jesus, the welcome mat to heaven has been placed on the front porch, and the light burns all night long.

There are two kinds of faces in the world: *yes* faces and *no* faces. A yes face is accepting, happy, compassionate and approachable. We love to be around yes faces and are irresistibly drawn to them. On the other hand, a no face is hard, judgmental, stiff and unapproachable. We tend to avoid them. When I think of Christ Jesus, I am quite certain that He had a yes face. Scripture says, "The common people heard him gladly" (Mark 12:37, KJV). When Jesus looked at you, His expression said, yes! The friendship principle we learn from Nympha is that of hospitality—wearing a yes face.

Paul: A Friend Who Holds You Accountable

A godly friend will care enough to tell you the truth—even when it hurts. Paul was just such a friend and did not hesitate to offer a corrective word to those he cared about. "Tell Archippus: 'See to it that you complete the work you have received in the Lord'" (Colossians 4:17, NIV). Some surmise that Archippus may have been a son to Philemon. Apparently, he had become slack in the calling God had placed on his life. Paul learned of it and sent him a loving rebuke.

This brief word of exhortation to Archippus is very similar to the message Paul sent to Timothy, his own son in the faith: "And the special gift of ministry you received when I laid hands on you and prayed—keep that ablaze!" (2 Timothy 1:6).

When I read these messages from Paul to his friends, it reminds me of Solomon's advice in Proverbs 27, which could almost be called "the friendship chapter" of Proverbs. The word *friend* is found six times in 27 verses. The first mention is found in the sixth verse: "Wounds from a friend can be trusted" (NIV). When a friend tells you something difficult to hear, you can always rest in the fact that it is spoken with the best of intentions. Verse six continues by drawing a contrast: "But the kisses of an enemy are lavish and deceitful" (AMPLIFIED). We will touch much more on the kisses of an enemy in part 2. Suffice it to say that loving gestures do not always spring from a genuine heart, but advice from a friend does.

> THE FRIENDSHIP PRINCIPLE WE LEARN FROM NYMPHA IS THAT OF HOSPITALITY— WEARING A YES FACE.

When I was in my early twenties and single, I had a tremendous zeal for ministry. I knew that I was called to minister God's Word and could not wait to get to it; so much so, in fact, that I dropped out of college (yup, the same one mentioned in chapter 2) in my junior year to pursue my calling. At the time, I had been serving as a college and career leader in my church with over five hundred young people under my spiritual care. And did I have vision! Television, radio, writing—and any other means of communication I could find—were on the radar

64

screen of my faith. *Next Billy Graham, here I come!* I thought.

Since my group had grown so large, I was certain that my local church home would bring me on board in a full-time position. Then I could really go for it! I set up an appointment with my pastor and walked into his office with a confident skip in my step. After I shared my vision, he asked, "Jeff, why did you quit school?" My pastor's steely eyes searched my face.

I was not prepared for the question. It completely took me off guard. Fumbling for words, I sputtered, "Well, Pastor, time is slipping by and I wanted to reach people for Christ now," his steady gaze making me increasingly uneasy.

"Jeff, I can't hire you full-time until you finish college. You're capable, bright and promising. I hate to see you let the opportunity pass you by."

My heart sank to the floor. Finish college? I felt like someone had punched me in the gut with an iron glove. Have you ever felt as if God wanted you to do something you really did not want to do; but until you did it, no other doors were going to open?

"But, Pastor, I don't even have the finances," I protested, hoping against hope it might change his mind. Then he said something that left me speechless.

"If you go, I will cover your tuition and books. Don't tell a soul or I'll withdraw my offer."

I was speechless. What could I say? There was no way out. Deeply humbled and moved, I thought: *This must be God.*

I took my pastor up on his offer, and he did just what he promised. Each semester I gave him the bill, and each semester he handed me a check made out to the school. I later obtained financial aid and finished my degree. I can tell you with all sincerity that I likely would have never finished my bachelor's degree nor gone on to finish graduate school if not for the "faithful wounds" of a friend who told me the truth.

To sum up, a godly friend

- fits into God's plan for us;
- obeys God under pressure;
- is loyal even when we fail;
- prays for us;
- is welcoming and hospitable; and
- holds us accountable.

But what do you do when someone you thought was a friend turns out otherwise? Or even worse, you discover that you were deceived into believing one thing about him or her, only to find that it was all a charade, a farce, a lie? Follow me to part 2 as we tackle the subject of deceivers.

PART 2

DECEIVERS

"Friend, why this charade?"
Matthew 26:50

4

THE GREAT PRETENDERS

At once Judas went straight to Jesus and said,
"Teacher!" and kissed Him.

Mark 14:45, NLV

The Judas Kiss

A well-known national correspondent for a major network was considered "Everyman" by the American public.
A short, bald, folksy fellow with a distinctive voice and
eloquent presentation, he was best known for covering odd-
ball stories in unusual, out-of-the-way places. His human-
interest stories made watching television on Sunday mornings a relaxing experience. But it turns out he kept perhaps
the juiciest story of all from his viewers.

Following his death in 1997, a woman completely unknown to his wife and family—then living in New York
City—filed a lawsuit in the Montana courts for the rights to
$600,000 worth of land and property near a fishing cabin

where she had spent decades—29 years to be exact—with the celebrated correspondent. Because of his job as a traveling journalist, Everyman had been free to play both sides of the romance fence. As the shocking truth unfolded, it was learned that he had given hundreds of thousands of dollars to his mistress and her children, to whom he was known as "Pop." Needless to say, his wife, on the heels of grieving over his death, had to face another death, the death of 29 years of a marriage that had never really been what she believed.

Stop and think about this a moment. *Twenty-nine years is a long time!* The pain of discovering all this following her husband's death, no doubt, was huge. Runaway imaginations mixed with the inability to ask questions, or to give vent to her well-deserved anger at the one who did this, would have leveled most women. This man was a deceiver. Without ever officially leaving, he had left, yet continued to act out the part of a married man. This was deception at a very high level. For virtually thirty years he lived a lie.

While this story involved a husband and wife, the principle of deception applies to all relationships, friendships included. Nothing hurts worse than to realize that someone you trusted has deceived you. Anger, hurt, confusion, humiliation, feeling like a fool; all are some of the throat-grabbing emotions we experience as the truth of deception and betrayal begins to dawn. "How could I have been so naïve, so blind, so stupid?" we ask ourselves. The deceiver may have been a business associate, a spiritual or political leader, a spouse or, alas, a friend. Either way, to discover that you were hoodwinked is tough to get over, to say the least.

I have dedicated this section to deception because, like you, I have come to realize that Christianity does not fix everything. Friends still hurt friends. And, like it or not, Christians still practice deception to varying degrees and fail to live up to the injunction found in Ephesians, "What this adds up to, then, is this: no more lies, no more pretense. Tell your neighbor the truth. In Christ's body we're all connected to each other, after all" (4:25). To be a "truth teller" within the context of friendship is key to its survival. But that takes work and resolve. By nature we humans do not care for confrontation, choosing the easier route of "smoothing things over" in order to avoid the issues that, if not worked through, will ultimately damage the friendship.

For instance, aside from being perhaps the most segregated hour of the week, some Sunday morning church services produce as much deception as a political convention. The minute we walk in the door, the charade begins. "Oh, Betty," we exclaim, "what a stunning dress!" when we are really thinking, *She must be preparing for Halloween early.* Or how about, "Pastor, that was an unforgettable message," when what we are really thinking is, *I will never forget how long thirty minutes seemed.*

The truth is that it is not wise or gracious to be truthful all the time. If we were, the entire Church would be embroiled in fisticuffs within a week! Friendships would cease to be, and most other relationships would never survive it. As a public speaker I can tell you, if you did not care for my message, at least sugarcoat the truth. As Jack Nicholson's character, Jessep, in *A Few Good Men* put it, "You can't handle the truth!" The truth is, most of us can't—not all of the time.

Since we all do it, when, then, is deception a sin? If to not be brutally truthful is actually a polite and loving thing to do in most cases, when is it wrong? One meaning of the word *deceive* from the Greek language is simply "to cheat."[1] That really says it all. Deception occurs when someone, the deceiver, lies or misleads in order to get what he or she knows could not be obtained through honesty. The used car salesman comes to mind, who tells a customer he is getting a great deal when, in fact, the car is worth half what he was told.

71

Deception is also used to cover up a transgression against an intimate relationship, such as marriage. When we discover this kind of deception, we say, "He (she) cheated on me!" In other words, we were led to believe something that was not true about the commitment level of the relationship. We invested our hearts in a lie. Pain, disillusionment and wounding are the result.

I like to call this the "Judas kiss." It is high-octane betrayal of the devastating kind when we lead someone's heart down the road of false promises and counterfeit feelings. The impact of this kind of deception on our well-being spikes the far end of the emotional Richter scale. Barring an inner healing from God, it carries the potential of lifelong wounding. Even Jesus faced the pain, heartache and disappointment of having been betrayed by someone very close to Him. Scripture tells us concerning Him: "We don't have a priest who is out of touch with our reality. He's been through weakness and testing, experienced it all—all but the sin" (Hebrews 4:15).

Jesus' own handpicked disciple, Judas Iscariot, while following Him from town to town, sleeping where He slept and sharing His persecutions, was secretly plotting to have Him killed. When Judas finally acted on his evil scheme, the Lord of glory was sold down the river for thirty pieces of silver. After receiving his dirty money, Judas led Roman soldiers to the place where Christ was resting with His disciples and kissed Him on the cheek. "Friend," Jesus responded, "why this charade?" (Matthew 26:50). In my book, this was the most heinous betrayal of all time. And with a kiss! That is like pouring acid into a wound.

Let's face it: A Judas kiss digs deeper than a root canal with ten times the pain. It shatters, humiliates, degrades and breaks your heart like little else can. It is not just that you were betrayed, but that you were betrayed with finesse, and by someone you had only been good to. Job knew of such pain and wrote, "My brothers have dealt deceitfully like a brook, like the streams of the brooks that pass away" (Job 6:15, NKJV).

Inner Vows

When deception and betrayal take place at this level of relationship, many make what John Sandford has called an inner vow. "Inner vows are determinations we make as children, determinations that become 'computer programs' within our nature. They energize our brains to reproduce repeatedly whatever the vow calls for."[2]

In other words, following a deeply wounding experience, we utter the familiar phrase, "Never again. That will never happen to me again." From then on, whether consciously or subconsciously, we order our lives to fall in line with the vow, manipulating circumstances and relationships accordingly. In short, deep within ourselves we make a covenant with the vow, *Never again*.

For instance, when I was a young teenager, it was extremely important to me to be accepted by the "popular" crowd. In my day the hippie movement was emerging, complete with bell-bottom jeans and, for the guys, long, flowing hair. I wanted desperately to be a part of all that and looked for friends accordingly. Scott fit the bill perfectly. He wore "cool" like a fragrant cologne; it just seemed to ooze out of him. You felt like someone special when you walked into a room next to Scott. He knew just how to carry himself, talk and play the part—sort of a Fonzie-type guy. Scott, I decided, was going to be my friend.

I had thought that Scott felt the same way about me. We had a great time when we were together. Natural chemistry seemed to flow between us. I recall waking up and being thrilled that I had developed this friendship with Mr. Cool himself.

One memorable night, Scott and I were supposed to do something together. At the last minute he phoned and said that something had come up having to do with his mother and he wouldn't be able to make it. Disappointed, I said, "Hey, man, it's okay. Give me a call tomorrow."

After hanging up, I decided to take in a movie at a theater where a bunch of us hung out. I threw on my coolest coat, combed my cool hair, and headed out. On arriving at the theater, I had just bought some popcorn and was walking through the lobby when I spotted—you guessed it—Mr. Cool himself. Scott was with a group of guys from school who were also part of the megacool crowd. He saw me at about the same time I saw him. The look on his face said it all. *Busted.* Rejection and humiliation washed over me like an emotional tsunami. He quickly turned away and walked into the movie with the other guys. That was it. End of relationship. Nothing more needed to be said.

> MANY OF THE WOUNDS THAT WE EXPERIENCE DELIVER A MESSAGE TO OUR SUBCONSCIOUS.

I left the theater feeling like Muhammad Ali had just hit me in the gut. As I already struggled with an inferiority complex, this had not helped. Deep down in the recesses of my soul I made a vow. *Never again.* I would never again leave myself open to that kind of pain, to feeling that stupid, that assaulted emotionally or that vulnerable to betrayal. As the rest of my teen years passed by, I kept that vow. As soon as a friendship would begin to grow close and I could feel myself growing attached to someone, a well-constructed wall would go up. One time I got cornered by a group of friends about this pattern in my life. "What's with you?" they wanted to know. "Why are you so distant?" Before I could think to edit my words, I blurted, "I don't need anyone!"

No one thought more about my outburst than I did. Suddenly I realized that a deep wound lay within me, and a great fear of being hurt that needed to be healed. With God's help over quite a long period of time, I was able to break the power of that inner vow and enjoy closer friendships—even if it did mean getting hurt from time to time.

Many of the wounds we experience deliver a message to our subconscious. It is the "message of the wound." You may not be fully aware of it, but it is there nevertheless. For all those years I had accepted the *message of my rejection*. "You're not lovable. No one will ever stay with you. Get used to it, because love means hurt and disappointment." And for years it worked.

Take, for instance, the little girl who does not receive her father's love and attention. In her deep wounding, a voice begins speaking: "You're not an attractive female. Men will never like you," the message of the wound whispers. Or, a young boy on a Little League baseball team is kept on the bench repeatedly. Dejected and wounded, he hears the voice speak: "You don't have it. You'll never amount to anything. You're a failure." The girl later experiences inexplicable and profound insecurity around men, and the boy never tries out for a team again, though he may be very gifted.

When we agree with and accept the false messages of our wounds, we are most vulnerable to uttering an inner vow. *Never again!* we shout within. *I'll never trust again, be hurt again, love again . . . never!* John and Stasi Eldredge explain why these false messages are so powerful: "Because they were delivered with such pain, they *felt* true."[3]

So, then, what do you think happens when a friendship we believe in fails us, particularly through deception and betrayal? Many utter the two words that forever turn the lock on the door of their hearts: "Never again."

Deception is as old as mankind itself. In fact, the Bible contains incredible stories that reveal some of the classic causes of deception and the bitter consequences it can bring. Let's explore a few.

It Was You!

Believe it or not, David the psalmist experienced heart-wrenching betrayals from friends. The book of Psalms is filled with moving, honest confessions of his experiences. A graphic blow-by-blow description of one betrayal is found in Psalm 55.

> This isn't the neighborhood bully mocking me—I could take that. This isn't a foreign devil spitting invective—I could tune that out. It's you! We grew up together! You! My best friend! Those long hours of leisure as we walked arm in arm, God a third party to our conversation.
>
> verses 12–14

Notice how he compares the pain a casual acquaintance *might* have caused to what a close friend *did* cause. He could have handled a bully or hateful individual with ease. But it was "you." It is easy to understand King David's dismay. We can feel him trying desperately to come to grips with *who* and *why*. The person he never thought would, *did*.

Another ingredient made David's ordeal even more confusing and painful. He continues: "Those long hours of leisure as we walked arm in arm, *God a third party to our conversation*" (italics mine). David's friendship had included a third party—God Himself. People of faith tend to believe that if a friendship is built around Christ, it will "betray-proof" and "deceit-proof" that relationship. Unfortunately, it does not. It may weaken the odds against such a tragedy; but human nature being what it is, no relationship is exempt.

David's betrayer was a man named Ahithophel, his long-time trusted counselor. Interestingly, his name means "brother of folly."[4] Ahithophel's wisdom and counsel were held in such high esteem that his advice carried the authority of a word straight from God. "The counsel that Ahithophel gave in those days was treated as if God himself had spoken. That was the reputation of Ahithophel's counsel to David" (2 Samuel 16:23).

Ahithophel chose to betray the king when David's own son Absalom led a revolt in a brazen attempt to seize the kingdom. In David's darkest hour, Ahithophel defected to Absalom's camp. This was industrial-strength betrayal, the double-edged sword, backstabbing, wipe-you-out-for-good-if-God-does-not-show-mercy kind.

Deceived and betrayed in the worst possible way at the worst possible time by the worst possible person. Ever experienced it? Are you dealing with such a betrayal as you read these pages? With friends like that, who needs enemies, right? Unfortunately, this happens all the time in churches, among Christians and between friendships as rich as David's had been. Why?

Deceivers deceive for varying reasons—for personal gain, to hide damaging or embarrassing truth, out of deep insecurity and sometimes even from pathology (as with a pathological liar). In the case of Ahithophel, it appears to have been motivated by several things. Power was likely one of them. "His name is the symbol of craftiness, cunning, faithlessness, cruelty, pride of intellect and ambition."[5]

But the underlying streams of even deeper motives ran through Ahithophel's soul, and here is where the plot thickens. David's confidant was likely driven by a root of bitterness from an event that had taken place around twelve years earlier. You see, Ahithophel was Bathsheba's grandfather. "Does not this fact explain why David's 'familiar friend' became his deadly foe, and account for his readiness to aid Absalom—thus seeking to avenge the dishonor brought upon his house?"[6]

David was out to conceal embarrassing, explosive information about himself; Ahithophel to exact revenge. Both men paid dearly for their deceiving ways. Ahithophel ultimately spiraled down to suicide. And David reaped the consequences of his actions within his own household for the rest of his life. No wonder Solomon warned, "He whose tongue is deceitful falls into trouble" (Proverbs 17:20, NIV).

A Liar and Two Weddings

Another incredible tale involves Rebekah, the patriarch Isaac's wife, who involved herself in perhaps the most brazen act of deception in the entire Old Testament. The story begins when she learns she is pregnant. As the pregnancy progressed, Rebekah knew instinctively that something about it was unusual. Inquiring of the Lord, she learned that two nations were in her womb; one nation would be stronger than the other, and the older child would serve the younger (see Genesis 25:23). The two boys would be called Jacob and Esau. Rebekah placed God's formidable promises in her "wait and see" file.

Scripture does not reveal whether Rebekah ever divulged to Isaac what God had told her about the older child serving the younger. We do know that she likely let Jacob in on it, for he made it his business to steal Esau's birthright by hook or crook. One day, following a particularly grueling hunting trip, Esau was on his way home when Jacob met him with a bowl of steaming stew in his hands. The irresistible odor wafted through the air like the fragrance from a Wonder Bread factory.

"Quick, let me have some of that red stew! I'm famished!" cried Esau (Genesis 25:30, NIV). I can almost picture the wily Jacob tantalizingly waving the bowl back and forth.

"Make me a trade: my stew for your rights as the first-born" (verse 31).

This was raw, unabashed manipulation. In a heartbreaking moment of weakness, Esau succumbed. Bingo! Jacob, whose name means "supplanter, or deceiver,"[7] was living up to his name.

The day arrived when Isaac, nearly blind and believing his days were numbered, asked Esau to go and retrieve some game for him. Esau would receive the blessing when he returned. Unbeknownst to them, Rebekah had been eavesdropping on the conversation. When she heard Isaac's promise to Esau, she hatched a scheme. One of the major differences between the two boys had been that Jacob was smooth-skinned, while Esau was hairy. So Rebekah commanded Jacob to kill some goats. She then dressed Jacob in Esau's clothes, took the skins of the goats he had killed and wrapped his hands and the smooth part of his neck with them.

With fresh venison in his hands, Jacob approached his unsuspecting father with the savory feast. "Who are you?" Isaac asked.

"I am Esau your firstborn. Here's the food, now please arise and bless me." Isaac inquired how in the world he got it so fast. "Because the LORD your God brought it to me." Now God had been brought in on the deception. Never a good idea.

"Please come near, that I may feel you, my son, whether you are really my son Esau or not." Feeling along with outstretched hands, his eyes staring into space, Isaac replied, "The voice is Jacob's voice, but the hands are the hands of Esau" (Genesis 27:20–22, NKJV).

By deceit, Jacob received Isaac's irrevocable blessing. The consequences quickly hit the fan. On learning of what had been done, Esau vowed that he would kill Jacob for it. But once again Mom stepped in to the rescue. She advised Jacob to flee to Haran to her brother Laban's house and stay for a few days. Little did either of them realize that a few days would become twenty years and that Jacob would never see his mother, Rebekah, alive again.

If Rebekah was good at trickery, her brother, Laban, was a master. Jacob ran like the wind to Haran. The first person he met was Laban's beautiful daughter, Rachel, who just happened to be drawing water from the well at which he first stopped. Cupid's arrow struck immediately. It was love at first sight. On meeting Laban, Jacob explained everything. Laban, a classic con artist, recognized a golden opportunity. Always on the hunt for extra laborers, the old pro struck a deal with Jacob: "Put in seven years for me, and I'll give Rachel as your wife." Fair enough! agreed the love-struck Jacob.

It is here that Scripture offers one of the best examples of the waiting power of true love: "So Jacob served seven years to get Rachel, but they seemed like only a few days to him because of his love for her" (Genesis 29:20, NIV). When the seven years were up, Jacob said to Laban, "Give me my wife, for my days are fulfilled, that I may go in to her" (verse 21, NKJV). Laban agreed and the wedding party commenced. What came down on the wedding night is mind-boggling. Either the Laban clan was serving up some very loaded punch at the feast or Jacob slept the night away on his honeymoon. The Bible records: "But in the morning [Jacob saw his wife, and] behold, it was Leah!" (verse 25, AMPLIFIED).

"Behold, it was Leah"? (Leah, by the way, was Rachel's less attractive older sister who also loved Jacob.) But, c'mon! Even if all the candles were blown out and it was pitch dark in the old wedding tent honeymoon suite, how do you not at least recognize an unfamiliar voice? And wouldn't Leah have been complicit in the deception every time Jacob said, "Rachel, my darling"? (And we thought modern soap operas had the edge on convoluted melodrama!)

Laban's response to a furious Jacob the next morning was classic: "And he said to Laban, What is this you have done to me? Did I not work for you [all those seven years] for Rachel? Why then have you deceived and cheated and thrown me down [like this]?" (verse 25, AMPLIFIED). Laban caustically replied, "We don't do it that way in our country. . . . We don't marry off the younger daughter before the older. Enjoy your week of honeymoon, and then we'll give you the other one also. But it will cost you another seven years of work" (verses 26–27).

Talk about what goes around comes around! The relentless hounds of sowing and reaping had found their man. Notice the uncanny similarities between Jacob's experience and what he had brought on Esau.

- Jacob had tempted Esau with something irresistible to get what he wanted—the birthright. Laban tempted Jacob with something irresistible, his daughter Rachel, to get what he wanted—seven years of free labor.
- Spurred by his mother, Jacob deceived his father, Isaac, by assuming a false identity. Spurred by Laban, Leah deceived Jacob by assuming a false identity.
- Isaac and Esau lived with the stinging pain of having been deceived for many long years. Jacob lived with the same stinging pain for seven long years.
- Isaac and Esau were deceived by Jacob, a family member. Jacob was deceived by Laban and Leah, family members.

I have looked closely at this story in order to illustrate a truth that I myself have needed reassurance of from time to time: Deceivers never get away with it. Even if they are not found out in the public arena, the inescapable law of sowing and reaping will track them down.

The Cost of Deception

Ahithophel practiced deception in order to wreak vengeance. King David succumbed to deception and murder to cover up his sin. Jacob fell into deception to get something he wanted. Deception seems to have just been a way of life for Laban, yet he still lost his family when Jacob returned

81

to the Promised Land. Each of these great pretenders paid a hefty, costly price.

But the major difficulty one encounters following the discovery of deceit and betrayal is the struggle with bitterness, with what it did to *you*. It is natural to want to see justice divvied out. *Surely they're not going to get away with this?* we wonder. I know this sounds formulaic and a bit preachy, but becoming a victim of deception and betrayal provides a great opportunity to learn how to lean on what Scripture teaches rather than on our own emotions. What matters most is your getting through it, not them "getting theirs." Allow me to provide a few words of encouragement and instruction before moving on to chapter 5, where we will explore this concept more deeply.

- *God saw it*: "GOD doesn't miss a thing—he's alert to good and evil alike" (Proverbs 15:3).
- *He will handle it*: "Don't insist on getting even; that's not for you to do. 'I'll do the judging,' says God. 'I'll take care of it'" (Romans 12:19).
- *Do not get in God's way. He does not need or want your help with vengeance*: "But leave the way open for [God's] wrath" (Romans 12:19, AMPLIFIED).
- *Practice forgiveness* (much more on this in chapter 6): "Make allowance for each other's faults, and forgive anyone who offends you. Remember, the Lord forgave you, so you must forgive others" (Colossians 3:13, NLT).
- *Decide to move forward*: "Forgetting what is behind and straining toward what is ahead" (Philippians 3:13, NIV).
- *Dare to risk friendship again*: "For God has not given us a spirit of fear and timidity, but of power, love, and self-discipline" (2 Timothy 1:7, NLT).

In the presence of a deep wounding, the choice is ours. We can choose to live in disillusionment, accepting the message of the wound, or move on to what God has planned. David moved on and finished out his kingly reign. Jacob, too, moved on and was renamed *Israel*, which means, "having power with God." Isaac moved on. Esau reconciled with Jacob and moved on. Following the abysmal treatment he had received from his friends, Job moved on into twice the blessing he had known before. The focus of Scripture more times than not is to point out how its varying characters moved past pain, regret, heartache and bitterness into God's greater plan.

The good news in all of this is that Scripture promises that God never wastes a pain. Not the slightest hurt or heart-wrenching experience sneaks past God's ever-restoring, ever-healing hands. Anything and everything is made to serve the ultimate tapestry He is weaving into our lives (see Romans 8:28). In the next chapter, let's take a look at how our difficult experiences can work for our good.

5

MORNING MIRRORS
TELL NO LIES

If you think you are too good for that,
you are badly deceived.

Galatians 6:3

Urban legend has it that when Leonardo da Vinci
began painting *The Last Supper*, he sought models
with faces that expressed his concept of the particular man he was focusing on at that moment. Known
for his relentless perfectionism, the artistic genius took on
the arduous task of finding exactly the right faces. While
attending mass one day, da Vinci spotted a young man of
striking features. Love, kindness, honesty and innocence
exuded from the countenance of one Pietro Bandinelli.
This would be his Christ!

After years of labor and close to finishing his masterpiece,
the time finally arrived to find the model who would best
exemplify Judas Iscariot, the traitor. Da Vinci searched far
and wide for that one particular face exquisitely etched

with greed, deceit, evil and disloyalty. Finally, he came upon a man in prison who bore all these qualities. At last, Judas! After obtaining permission to use the prisoner as a model, Leonardo began painting in earnest. As the days wore on, he noticed signs of sadness, anguish and distress on the prisoner, who just could not seem to quit staring at the canvas. "What is troubling you so much?" Leonardo asked. The man suddenly began to sob, burying his face in his hands. Finally, he looked up and said to Leonardo, "Don't you remember me? Years ago I was your model for the Christ!" Having lost his way in a life of crime, sin had left its signature on his once beautiful face.

While this is, no doubt, urban legend, there is a truth behind the myth. We all have the potential to be a Judas: to betray, to deceive, to turn our backs on people who care for us, to play the charade game. Because we, too, are in a fallen state. In fact, precious few can attest to never having administered at least a few Judas kisses of their own. It is hard to admit this, especially when you are in the throes of spitting fire and brimstone in the direction of those who have deceived and betrayed you.

This particular brand of trial—brought on by betrayal— has almost always produced in me a season of deep soul-searching. Unfortunately, I am just not inclined to such when things are going well because, well, things are going well! But the "horrible pit" and "miry clay," so well described by David in Psalm 40:2 (NKJV), have a way of placing a mirror in front of my face and saying, "Take a good, hard, long look at yourself."

Nothing will position you for change greater than pain. Pain has its advantages. God never wastes a pain, and neither should you. What you see in the mirror when friendship has hit the rocks, the curtain has closed and only you remain in the presence of a very probing God, is valuable. I call it the *morning mirror* (I suppose we could call it the *mourning* mirror) because morning mirrors never lie.

If all you do following the harsh revelation of having been duped is shoot red-hot arrows at the one who deceived you, you are missing a chance to grow. Forget them. They are gone! *It is time for you.* Every failed relationship offers an opportunity to spring back better and stronger, but to do so takes courage because it will require being open to the areas in which you may have failed. It is easy to play the blame game. It is hard to learn and grow.

We are frequently very dishonest about ourselves *to* ourselves. Ever noticed that? Frankly, we can choose to live with all kinds of lies when it has to do with ourselves. It is so very comforting and safe to live in denial. This is why self-honesty must often be preceded by either a shattering, heartbreaking, even traumatic event, or by the penetration of God's mighty Word into our souls. Only then are we willing to allow the bright light of truth to penetrate our self-righteous veils.

Even in the physical arena we are overwhelmingly cosmetic, spending billions annually to cover up our flaws. Few among us are willing to jump out of bed and head straight for the office before engaging in some form of cover-up. For me, the morning mirror is brutally truthful. Take your pick—the bags under the eyes that look like someone injected you with Botox in all the wrong places, wrinkles etched into whichever side of your face you slept on, the matted hair, the encroaching crows' feet, those erring zits that somehow have not been informed you are no longer a teen . . . shall I go on?

The Morning Mirror Is Brutally Truthful

It is during the times of relationship failure that our own character flaws are most visible. And it is also in these times that we are most liable to play the blame game and shine the glaring light of accusation on someone else. It has always struck me as humorous that Adam and Eve immediately began to blame each other for their own failure, even bringing the devil into it, conjuring echoes of Flip Wilson's famous "the devil made me do it" slogan (see Genesis 3:11–13). It took God addressing them both individually to place the responsibility where it lay. Eve had failed Adam by eating the forbidden fruit. And Adam failed Eve and the entire human race by entering into her sin. The very first consequence of sin was broken relationships, both with God and with each other, and it has been the same ever since.

God uses those dark seasons of the soul following a relationship failure to place the morning mirror squarely before us so that we might do some soul-searching. "Examine your motives, test your heart," the Bible advises (1 Corinthians 11:28). Like it or not, it is the valley times, the burning, fiery oven times, the drop-back-and-punt times, the *I don't know what to do anymore* times that produce the greatest spiritual growth. It is then that we are uniquely open to seeing what needs to change.

Not too long ago, I passed through the darkest hour of my life. It involved a personal relationship failure, betrayal on the part of people I thought were lifelong friends and great loss. I discovered during this time that many of the people who had been standing beside me were not standing *with* me. There is a difference. What made a dark situation even darker was that when I was down for the count, the people who had been around Cathy and me, many of whom made their living off of what we had built in obedience to Christ, turned on us, caring far more about what we had built than about us. I now know what it feels like to be misrepresented, slandered and forgotten. It was a gut-wrenching, life-altering experience, with "friends" not being what we thought.

I am certain that if I had not known how to lay hold of God through His Word and prayer, it would have spelled the permanent end of everything I hold dear. Without question, this was the enemy's plan. In my desperation, I arose each morning at the break of day, grabbed my Bible along with Matthew Henry's commentary (my favorite) and went out onto my patio. For hours on end I would soak in the Scriptures, allowing them to build my faith, ignite hope and strengthen my soul. I literally was fighting for my spiritual life, and I knew it.

During this deep valley, I purchased a little outdoor fountain that I placed near my chair. It was comforting to hear the gentle gurgle of the water, like sitting near a calming stream. One day my wife came back from the store with a small, smooth rock that had the word *hope* painted on it, which I placed at the top of the fountain so that the water rushed over it first as it made its way down to the bottom. *Hope.* I positioned my chair so that it was in my constant line of vision. I needed to see it. To hear it. To believe it.

Meanwhile, I began to discover in a fresh, new way that the Word of God is like the morning mirror that unapologetically reflects the true condition of our heart and soul. It reveals our flaws and shortcomings so that we might change, rather than try to cover them up. "Those who hear and don't act are like those who glance in the mirror, walk away, and two minutes later have no idea who they are, what they look like" (James 1:23–24).

James' point is this: It does you and me no good at all if, on seeing our flaws, weaknesses and sins reflected in the mirror of God's Word, we forget what we saw. When that happens we have wasted our time and missed out on a golden opportunity to grow.

Get the picture? Each time we open the pages of Scripture we are in essence holding a mirror up to our soul. It always tells the truth about two things—*God* and *you*. If you want to know what God is like, read the Bible. If you want to know what you are like, read the Bible. The Word of God is like a divine scalpel, and Christ is the surgeon.

For the word of God is alive and powerful. It is sharper than the sharpest two-edged sword, cutting between soul and spirit, between joint and marrow. It exposes our innermost thoughts and desires.

Hebrews 4:12, NLT

For instance, suppose you open up the Scriptures one morning and read the following verse: "Do not take revenge, my friends, but leave room for God's wrath, for it is written: 'It is mine to avenge; I will repay,' says the Lord" (Romans 12:19, NIV). *Wow!* you think. *God will take care of my enemies! What a powerful truth!* You close the Bible, head out the door and notice a neighbor whom you know has recently bad-mouthed you walking down the sidewalk. But rather than giving him or her over to God as you just read, you approach and soundly kick him or her in the shins. The glance into the morning mirror of God's Word has done you no good at all. The way you live was not changed.

As my slow, painful process of restoration progressed, I noticed that part of God's dealings involved gently pointing out things that needed to change in me. It ceased being about others—those who had betrayed and deceived me—and instead focused on my part. I would have never seen this when times were good. But now, in the valley of the shadow, desperate for healing and help, I was open. As always, the mirror was hard to face. But in order to be restored, I had to listen to God's Word and that still small voice of the Holy Spirit.

As days became weeks and weeks stretched into months, God undertook some heavy-duty rearranging in the rooms of my soul. While dedicating my life to helping others, I had at times also been proud, presumptuous and self-centered. Gently, ever so gently, the morning mirror reflected the blemishes and wrinkles that needed to go.

Did this mean that others had not done wrong? No. But that was not the issue as I journeyed toward wholeness. It reminds me of the time when Jesus informed Peter of the way he would one day die. It was not pretty, and it sure did not make Peter's day.

> "I'm telling you the very truth now: When you were young you dressed yourself and went wherever you wished, but when you get old you'll have to stretch out your hands while someone else dresses you and takes you where you don't want to go." He said this to hint at the kind of death by which Peter would glorify God.
>
> John 21:18–19

John, who recorded this story, was standing nearby. Rather than accepting it, Peter's initial response to this prediction of his future martyrdom was to focus on John and say, "Not fair! What about him?"

> Turning his head, Peter noticed the disciple Jesus loved following right behind. When Peter noticed him, he asked Jesus, "Master, what's going to happen to him?"
>
> verses 20–21

Jesus' response is something we who have been betrayed and deceived and are seeking inner healing must hear. "If I want him to remain alive until I return, what is that to you? You must follow me" (verse 22, NIV).

In time, I began to accept that those who had wronged me were not mine to deal with. They must and will answer to God for their part. The positive aspect to my experience was the changes God was bringing into my own life. Each time I caught myself growing angry, regurgitating past events, rehearsing all the ways *they* had done wrong and wondering why seemingly nothing had happened to them when I had paid such a high price, God would whisper, *What is that to you? You follow Me.*

There has got to come a time when we release into God's hands people who have hurt us and cut the string. When Peter urged, "Casting all your care upon Him, for He cares for you" (1 Peter 5:7, NKJV), he was not thinking of a fisherman with a rod and reel, who casts his bait then slowly reels it back. That is what I had been doing: reeling it all back. Now, I have learned to cut the line and leave it with Him.

An Incredible Promise

There is a verse that has carried and kept me sane during my toughest experiences. You probably know it well yourself: "And we know that in all things God works for the good of those who love him, who have been called according to his purpose" (Romans 8:28, NIV).

Perhaps the Roman Christians to whom Paul addressed his letter knew this statement to be true, but, honestly, I wondered what exactly it meant when I just could not see any light at the end of the tunnel. I mean, it sounds so easy, so black and white. Do we only need to place a great big problem in God's outstretched hands, and *poof!* like a divine magician rolling a coin around in His palms, it is gone? I wondered just how God could work everything out for my good when all that remained was a pile of smoldering ashes.

Tennis Talks

Two longtime friends, to whom I will always be grateful, stuck with me through all this mess—Tony the pilot and Frank the fireman. Tony flies for FedEx and has been my racquetball and tennis partner for years. I am also his pastor. One day as winter was giving way to a gorgeous spring, Tony and I were sitting on a bench huffing and puffing after a tennis game. Guys are not like girls. We do not easily venture into the land mine–laden fields of talking about personal pain, as a rule. It is usually more like one guy will say, "How you doin'?" to which the typical reply will be driven by a fear of revealing any sign of weakness. "Oh, couldn't be better. Wife's great. Kids are great. Work's great. God is good!" Usually, at least, partial lies.

Tony and I had succeeded in getting past this shallow level of communicating through years of getting busted up by different trials and tribulations in front of each other. Once you bleed in front of a friend, it is easier from then on to just tell the truth. After a minute of silence, Tony shot the usual question,

"So, how you doing?"

"Oh, I'm doing okay," I said, bouncing a tennis ball up and down with my racquet. "Just forging ahead. That's really all you can do, right?" I asked, glancing his way.

"Man, I've gotta tell you; I don't know how you've done it, Jeff. I don't think I could have survived all of this," he honestly replied.

Thinking about that for a minute, I said, "You know, Tony, if I hadn't believed in God and, in particular, Romans 8:28, I think I would have lost my mind. I just have to believe that God is working through it all; sort of behind the scenes in ways we cannot see. I mean, isn't that the promise?"

Tony thought a minute. "Yeah, I suppose that's true. But even so, wow. . . . " His voice trailed off in reflection.

"Well," I continued, "I can tell you that it's all made me look at my own heart more than usual. Like, what can I learn from all this so that it's not just a total train wreck; so that some good comes out of it, you know?" I stood up and grabbed a cup of water, knowing we were not finished knocking around this "everything works out for your good" issue.

"Okay," said Tony, "do you see anything yet that's working for your good? Is God talking to you?"

I thought a moment and said, "Yes, He is." Sitting up straight and waxing more serious, I continued, "Seeking

God out on my patio at the crack of dawn with my Bible and Matthew Henry's commentary, digging through them both for my very life, I have begun to catch a glimpse of something I have never really focused much on: *the sovereignty of God*. What I mean is, the stunning, incredible realization that God is in charge of His universe. He is never checkmated by the devil, and He never says, 'Oops!' or, 'Well I'll be.' Just like Jesus predicted Peter's denial, He knows the mistakes we will make before we make them. But the incredible news is, because He is God, He can take what the enemy meant for evil and turn it for our good. The psalmist says that He can even make the wrath of man praise Him" (see Psalm 76:10).

Again, Tony pushed, "Well then, give me a way, besides your realizing that God is sovereign over problems, that this mess is working for your good."

"Okay," I began, staring at the ground and letting the bouncing tennis ball roll away. "I had a lot of pride, Tony. I realize that now. I was also presumptuous, taking a lot of God's blessings for granted, just assuming they would always be there. There were some attitudes that were wrong. Rather than being thankful for what I *did* have, I focused on what wasn't there and allowed those things to shoot me down."

"Yeah," said Tony the pilot, "that's easy to do. I guess we all do that sometimes."

I went on, "The Scriptures have become like a mirror, revealing all the blemishes, zits and wrinkles of my soul. And there were plenty. But mercifully and gently, God has shown me the stuff that needs to change and has assured me that, in ways I can't see, He's working things out for my good. And"—I breathed deeply here—"I know He's not finished with me yet."

"Man," said Tony, "I just can't believe what some of those people did. *That* would be my hurdle."

About then a couple of ladies walked in and took the court next to us, wondering why we were just sitting there.

It did not matter; this was important guy talk, so we just kept going. "Like I said, if I didn't believe that God was working on my behalf, it would all have driven me crazy. But I know that the only way through something like this is the narrow way Jesus talked about: the way of forgiveness, of confession, of honesty with myself and God and of seeking Him hard every day. It's a narrow way because it's restrictive and exclusive; it is mono-optional, His way or no way. In the Lord's Kingdom, Tony, the way up is down, down in humility and honesty. Breakthroughs start coming after that like drops of mercy after a long drought." Tony nodded in his quiet way, and we called it a day.

"Darn!" I said out loud. Driving home that day, I realized that I had forgotten to bring up the second part of Romans 8:28 in my discussion with Tony, the part about *purpose*. God not only promises to work out all things for the good of His children, even bad things, but the verse also tells us *why* He does this: to bring about His purpose for us. Christians are those "who have been called according to his purpose." And what is that purpose? The next verse tells us: "For those God foreknew he also predestined to be conformed to the likeness of his Son" (verse 29, NIV).

Because of verses like this one, God began to change my thinking about how I viewed trials and even salvation. Our salvation is not just about eternal security, as if we took out some kind of insurance policy with State Farm in order to miss hell and gain heaven. God's purpose is far greater than this. One of the most mind-blowing verses in the entire Bible has got to be the one that says, "Long before he laid down earth's foundations, he had us in mind" (Ephesians 1:4). Can you even begin to wrap your mind around that?

In essence, long before God commanded the light to shine, before a countless parade of birds graced the ancient blue sky, the first lion shattered the silence with his kingly roar or giant whales rolled and glided through a primeval sea; when "Earth was a soup of nothingness, a bottomless emptiness, an inky blackness" (Genesis 1:2), God was thinking of you with a *purpose* on His mind. "For whom He foreknew, He also predestined to be conformed to the image of His Son" (Romans 8:29, NKJV).

God's ultimate purpose is for us to be fashioned into the image of His Son. And according to verse 28, *everything* that happens *to* us, *for* us, *in* us, *around* us and *through* us will be bent to serve that purpose, including the pain inflicted by those who hurt us. "If God says, 'All things,'" writes Chuck Swindoll, "He means just that."[1]

Later that week I talked to my other friend, Frank the fireman, and got the chance to mull this over with him. Frank was one of the few people in my circle who acted like Jesus when everything hit the fan. He called regularly to check on me and was one of those rare individuals willing to take calls at two in the morning without being bugged. Sometimes I even called him at the firehouse when I could hear stuff banging around, like maybe a fire had happened. During one of those late night calls, I told him, "The only thing keeping me sane, Frank, is that I know God's purpose for me still stands, and that His purpose is bigger than this trial."

"Pastor," he replied, "we know that things are already starting to turn. God has not been hoodwinked by any of this. You are doing the right thing. Just keep seeking Him and walk in obedience because, yes, His calling and purpose for your life are intact."

I knew while talking with him that Frank is not a theologian, he is a fireman. He cannot traipse through Greek any more than I could walk into a raging fire and know how to put it out. Aware that I could have wandered off into all of the theological profundities of election, purpose, predestination and so on, it struck me that what I really needed was already there in my midnight hour: an accessible, listening, encouraging and *present* friend. When so many others had walked away, Frank the fireman walked in and was a crucial link between Jesus and me.

At around 2:30 that morning, Frank said one more thing before hanging up. "I can't fanthom (that is how Frank says *fathom*) what everyone involved was thinking, what their motives were, though some are pretty clear now. But the important thing is that *you* keep doing the right thing, that *you* keep obeying Him. Remember, Pastor, God is in control."

As I hung up and sat alone in my study, I thought, *If God had a purpose for me before time began, and decreed by His sovereign might that it would be done, I will do my best not to insult Him by thinking otherwise.* About then God seemed to speak these words to my heart in the still of the night: *Give Me time. Watch how My providence works. When you don't understand My hand, trust My heart.*

> ABOUT THEN GOD SEEMED TO SPEAK THESE WORDS TO MY HEART IN THE STILL OF THE NIGHT: *GIVE ME TIME. WATCH HOW MY PROVIDENCE WORKS. WHEN YOU DON'T UNDERSTAND MY HAND, TRUST MY HEART.*

If I had not believed that promise in Romans, clung to it, read it over and over, memorized it, reminded myself of it and held God to it in prayer, my trials would have been my undoing. I now understand better David's statement as he wondered, "[What, what would have become of me] had I not believed that I would see the Lord's goodness in the land of the living!" (Psalm 27:13, AMPLIFIED).

Through the mirror of God's Word we can experience transformation into His likeness. With that hope alive, even the pain of having been deceived and betrayed will be made to serve our good. There is one thing, however, that can hinder the transformation process, and you really need to know about it. Follow me to the next chapter as we crawl through the barbed wire of offense and find the power to forgive.

6

CRAWLING THROUGH
BARBED WIRE

"And forgive us our sins, as we have forgiven
those who sin against us."

Matthew 6:12, NLT

Julius Caesar viewed Marcus Junius Brutus as his protégé.
Brutus may even have been his son, Caesar having had a
long affair with Servilia, Brutus's mother. The two men
knew each other intimately, having enjoyed the fruits of
political power together. On the famous Ides of March, 44
BC, Caesar entered the Roman Senate house for a meeting
as scheduled. Suddenly, he was confronted with a band
of assassins. Initially, he struggled to escape, fighting as
best he could. Then he saw his comrade, Brutus, step out
of the shadows holding a glistening dagger. Shocked by
betrayal, he dropped his hands and uttered the famous
words, *"Et tu, Brute?"* translated, "You too, Brutus?" and
fought no longer.

You know you have come upon a betrayal that will take some getting over when there is a *"you too?"* involved. Caesar had one thing going for him—he never had to face his betrayer again. But for those who must move on with life following deception and betrayal, the challenge becomes what to do with the anger, resentment and pain. Someone you thought never would, did. A friend, spouse, comrade-in-arms, close co-worker, parent or child steps from the shadows as your unexpected betrayer. "You too?" we cry aloud. This is not only a knife in the back. It is a red-hot one. Not only must we deal with the reality of deception and betrayal, but also with *whom* the betrayal involved.

Fred, a good friend of mine, employed a young man who became like a son to him. He took "Steve" under his wing and mentored him, teaching him practically everything he knew about his business. Steve gave every appearance of being grateful for the opportunity to learn, as well as for the friendship that developed between the two men. They, along with their wives, often went out together. The couples also attended the same church.

Then two bombs were dropped like nukes on the friendship in rapid succession. First, Steve unceremoniously and with no warning quit. Second, Fred learned that Steve had gone to work for a competitor, one who had been openly critical of Fred.

The knife was turned again when Fred learned that Steve had been secretly courting his new employer, criticizing Fred and his business behind his back. *You too?*

I mentioned earlier that *response is the key to survival.* The right response in this situation was never more important. If you let it, such an event can cripple you for life, robbing you of your joy and stealing your peace. Because of this danger, the Son of God pulled no punches when dealing with the universal problem of bitterness.

"If you forgive those who sin against you, your heavenly
Father will forgive you. But if you refuse to forgive others,
your Father will not forgive your sins."

Matthew 6:14–15, NLT

In all honesty, I do not like the idea that my right standing before God hinges on forgiving others. Can't we just
ask God to forgive us and, well, sweep our feelings toward
others under the carpet? I have tried walking around this
difficult passage, but it is like circling a cul-de-sac—you
keep coming back to the same old truth. We must forgive
others to keep our relationship with God intact.

This brings a lot of pressure to bear on the sticky issue
of forgiveness. There is probably nothing harder than to
respond to enemies the way Christ taught us to. It has certainly proven so for me. I wish I could tell you that I have
mastered the art of forgiveness. Nope, not even close. For
me, it is sort of like trying to crawl through barbed wire
every time. I am much more inclined to remember the stuff I
should forget and to forget the things I should remember.

Sigmund Freud once mused that we should forgive our
enemies, but not before they have been hanged. To forgive
runs completely contrary to our natural inclinations. Left to
ourselves, we might as well be required to drink a glass full
of castor oil than be required to forgive someone who has
deeply hurt us. Several obstacles immediately leap to the
fore when forgiveness is mentioned. A few come to mind:

- We do not think the offender deserves it.
- We believe that our anger and bitterness are somehow giving the offender the punishment he or she
  deserves.
- We fear that if we do not punish him or her, he or she is
  going to walk away scot-free of any consequences.
- We do not *feel* like forgiving. Programmed to act upon
  feelings, we fail to forgive.

101

- We fear that forgiving our offender will reopen a painful, even destructive relationship. To not forgive, we conclude, keeps him or her at arm's length.

Let's remove some of these obstacles to forgiveness. First, forgiveness has absolutely nothing to do with what someone deserves. Forgiveness is called forgiveness because we are called upon to forgive someone who has definitely hurt us. It may have been something as minor as a misspoken word, all the way up to the tragedy of sexual abuse or some other major transgression. So let's be clear, forgiveness is what we as Christians are commanded to do when we have been wronged, period.

Christ taught that we must forgive because God has forgiven us. If everyone got what they deserved, there would be no human beings left on the planet. The rub comes in while fighting intense feelings *not* to forgive. Forgiveness for me has virtually never been feeling-driven. Forgiveness, I have found, is fueled by obedience. As Philip Yancey wrote: "It is much easier to act your way into feelings than to feel your way into actions."[1] We are to practice forgiveness because we all at some point need forgiveness. Not a day goes by that I do not find myself in need of God's forgiveness for a thought, a misspoken word, a wrong action or a negative attitude.

In Jesus' striking parable of an unforgiving servant, we find a man whose master, the king, had forgiven him much debt but who would not, in turn, forgive his own servant, who likewise owed him money (see Matthew 18:23–35). God, represented by the king, was angry.

> "Then the king called in the man he had forgiven and said, 'You evil servant! I forgave you that tremendous debt because you pleaded with me. Shouldn't you have mercy on your fellow servant, just as I had mercy on you?'"
>
> Matthew 18:32–33, NLT

This parable presents the primary reason for all forgiveness: because we, too, have received such amazing forgiveness from God. Paul chimes in, advising, "Be kind and compassionate to one another, forgiving each other, just as in Christ God forgave you" (Ephesians 4:32, NIV).

In Jesus' parable, the man who was forgiven first owed 10,000 talents. A talent was the largest unit of accounting in the Greek currency and was worth 10,000 denarii. In Jesus' time, a denarius was the daily wage of a laborer.[2] A daily wage times 10,000 equaled the value of one talent, or, 10,000 workdays would earn you a talent. If you were to divide the average annual 260 working days into 10,000, you arrive at 38.46 years. A talent, then, was equivalent to a lifetime of working. The first man owed 10,000 talents. Jesus knew that He was describing a hopeless debt representing 10,000 lifetimes!

> FORGIVENESS HAS ABSOLUTELY NOTHING TO DO WITH WHAT SOMEONE DESERVES.

On the other hand, the man's servant owed only 100 denarii, or 100 days of labor. Easily doable. But the man who was forgiven 10,000 lifetimes of labor refused to forgive even 100 denarii of debt. It is easy to see what Christ was driving at. When we stop to consider just what God has forgiven us of, it is sobering. Ours was a hopeless, nonnegotiable debt of sin represented as 10,000 lifetimes worth in its scope! We could never have paid it off. Bankrupt, and without any way of settling the account, humanity was at the mercy of the Master.

The man who owed 100 denarii represents the sins we commit against each other. Jesus was informing us that, no matter what we do to one another, it cannot come close to the sin debt we owed to God. *And He forgave us.* How absurd, then, to refuse to forgive one another when we have been forgiven the equivalent of 10,000 lifetimes of sin debt to God.

This turns my thoughts to the well-known Christmas movie *It's a Wonderful Life*. The main character, George Bailey, realizes that, due to financial bungling on the part of his Uncle Billy, he owes the bank that he manages a debt he cannot possibly repay. In a spiral of depression, he decides that suicide is his only recourse. Of course, the movie takes a wonderful turn at this juncture when his guardian angel, Clarence, appears to reveal what the world would have been like had he never been born. At the end of the movie, George is transported back to the real world. Though thrilled to be back, his pressing debt remains. To his overwhelming surprise, friends and relatives who have learned of his dilemma flood his house, donating thousands of dollars to relieve the debt load. (If you can keep a dry eye at this point in the movie, you need prayer.)

Jesus did for us what George's loved ones did for him. *He paid a debt He did not owe, because we owed a debt we could not pay.* George would have gone to prison, but we would have perished forever in a Christ-less eternity. When you consider the staggering debt-load of sin that God forgave us through Christ, it seems rather ridiculous to take the position of unforgiveness toward others who, at their worst, could not possibly have done to us what our sins did to God.

No wonder the king in Jesus' parable responded as he did to the ungrateful man who would not likewise forgive another. "Then the angry king sent the man to prison to be tortured until he had paid his entire debt" (Matthew 18:34, NLT). I am convinced that the prison Christ mentions is real, though not of brick, mortar and steel. There is a prison where the unforgiving are confined. Bitterness has its own bars of steel. The world is filled with those who are imprisoned in self-imposed misery, sickness, depression and hopelessness due to the unwillingness to forgive. Jesus tagged His somber parable with a promise, but not one I care to experience. "That's what my heavenly Father will do to you if you refuse to forgive your brothers and sisters from your heart" (verse 35, NLT).

Only Hurting Yourself

Frank the fireman, like I said earlier, is not a theologian. But what he does know of the teachings of Jesus he holds onto like a pit bull. "You've got to forgive, Pastor Jeff. If you don't, God will not be able to take you forward, and you're only hurting yourself," he has said to me at least a thousand times. And I know it is true. Seeking to punish the offender by hanging on to bitterness only hurts you. The Bible teaches that sin is deceitful (see Hebrews 3:13). *Deceitful* comes from a Greek word meaning "that which gives a false impression, whether by appearance, statement or influence."[3] Sin's danger lies in its ability to camouflage itself, to not appear to be sin. It gives the false impression of offering a valid solution to a problem. Had it not been good at this, sin would have gone out of business long ago. Only when it successfully deceives us does sin succeed.

Harboring bitterness in order to hurt someone else makes about as much sense as swallowing strychnine in hopes of poisoning your enemy. I assure you, the person or persons you are nursing ill feelings toward are not suffering anything like you are. In fact, they have probably gone on with life and are hardly giving the matter a second thought. Experience has taught me that, over time, they simply process the events that transpired, piece it all together in their thinking so that you, not they, are the bigger culprit and move on unruffled. When an encounter takes place at work, at church or on the street, and you give them your best laser beam—"you filthy dog, you scum of the earth, how can you sleep at night, God's gonna get you" look—that, too, will wear thin as their defense systems process it all in their favor. And where do you end up? Angry, depressed and defeated.

God Will Have His Say—*If You Let Him*

I know what you are probably thinking. *You mean they just walk away scot-free? No consequences, no price to pay, nothing? Not fair! I want justice!* This is where the proverbial rubber of your faith meets the road of unfair life. What to do? There is hardly a more difficult arena for our Christianity to be tested than the requirement to forgive and leave those who have hurt us to God. Remember, your response is far more important than what happened to you. I want you to listen very carefully to the following verses; they may save you many a tearful and sleepless night. "Do not say, 'I'll pay you back for this wrong!' Wait for the LORD, and he will deliver you" (Proverbs 20:22, NIV). *The Message* phrases it this way: "Don't insist on getting even; that's not for you to do. 'I'll do the judging,' says God. 'I'll take care of it'" (Romans 12:19).

Sounds easy, right? Nope. *It is a struggle to believe that God really will take care of it.* It was this very issue that prompted many of my late night calls to Frank. Often, I had absolutely nothing new to say, but was trying to come to grips with this whole issue of not taking vengeance, to get it from my head down into my heart of hearts. "Did He really see what happened to me?" I would ask. "If He did, is He really going to do something about it? And if so, when? It's been a week, and they haven't met with disaster yet!"

Sometimes I wondered if Frank had nodded out on me. Things would get quiet, and I could picture him lying there with the phone sitting next to his ear, "sawing logs." But always the trouper, he would come around and repeat the same truth, patiently helping me wrap my faith around it. Some of the things we nailed down are the familiar roadblocks we all encounter when trying to leave an offender in God's hands. Here are a few of them.

First roadblock: We expect God to deal with the situation in a particular *way*. Let's be honest about this. We want them to suffer. Do not polish your halo too quickly as you read these words. You know what you have thought about in your moments of hottest anger and deepest struggles. We want God to do what we would do if *we* were God. Right? We want visible results. When He does not handle it *our* way, we conclude He is not handling it at all.

This brings to mind the story of Jesus' journey toward Jerusalem as He was approaching the cross (see Luke 9:51–56). On the way, He entered a city of the Samaritans. When the occupants saw that His face was set for the holy city, they did not receive Him. When two of His disciples, James and John, heard about this, they made a very telling statement: "Lord, do You want us to command fire to come down from heaven and consume them, just as Elijah did?" (Luke 9:54, NKJV). Jesus responded with words we who are offended need to hear: "You do not know what manner of spirit you are of. For the Son of Man did not come to destroy men's lives but to save them" (verses 55–56, NKJV).

The disciples were offended at the way the Samaritans had treated Jesus. Note carefully their response. James and John wanted the entire town—men, women and children—vaporized! Puffs of smoke to the glory of God; grease spots on the streets of Samaria. An even scarier thought is that they, the sold-out disciples of Christ, wanted to be the ones to do it! They were unaware of the type of spirit they spoke out of. Though offended on behalf of Christ, they were not representing the *character* of Christ. Elijah had indeed called fire out of heaven, but not to consume people. The fire he brought down consumed only the sacrifice of wood and water that the priests of Baal had laid out in order that Elijah could show the superiority of Jehovah God over Baal (see 1 Kings 18).

This is why God is God, and why we are not. No doubt, whole churches and towns would have become puffs of smoke long ago had we held the power to call fire out of heaven. I hear an important message in this account. Jesus

107

was in essence saying, "The way I handle people is not the way *you* would. You're just going to have to trust Me." God spoke to this issue through the prophet Isaiah:

> "I don't think the way you think. The way you work isn't the way I work. For as the sky soars high above earth, so the way I work surpasses the way you work, and the way I think is beyond the way you think."
>
> Isaiah 55:8–9

The *second roadblock* we experience when turning our offenders over to God is a *timing* issue. We want them judged *yesterday*. The fact that God may take weeks, months or even years goes against our carnal grain. It helps enormously to understand that delay is not denial. God has a different calendar. He operates outside the realm of time. He is not staring at a watch or a clock. He is infinitely beyond us. The information He possesses of the whole stinky mess is so much greater than ours. Thus, He informs us, "I don't think the way you think."

> IT HELPS ENORMOUSLY TO UNDERSTAND THAT DELAY IS NOT DENIAL.

Because God sees every angle to the problem and knows the motives and thoughts of everyone involved, He will always work it out differently than we would. We are so inclined to humanize the Almighty that it helps to remind ourselves that He is not like us. "God is a Spirit," Jesus said (John 4:24, KJV). Speaking through Asaph, God contends, "You thought I was altogether like you. But I will rebuke you" (Psalm 50:21, NIV).

It is actually a relief to realize that only God can fulfill the job description for deity. Paul the apostle, a brilliant master theologian, whose mind went where most of ours will never go, concluded that God's ways are *past finding out* (see Romans 11:33). If given the opportunity to study

God's ways for a thousand years, we would never plumb the depths of why He does some of what He does. It is past finding out. As I have grown in my faith, I have come to accept this. I do not have all the answers. To just admit, "I don't understand this, but that's okay," can bring such peace. Speaking of God's judgments, Paul concedes that they are *unsearchable*, confessing that on our best day, "We see things imperfectly as in a cloudy mirror" (1 Corinthians 13:12, NLT).

It is not that everything about God is mysterious, unknowable and unfathomable. We can and do understand many things about Jehovah God, such as His love, mercy, justice, patience and gentleness. But these things are only what He has chosen to reveal to us in His Word. Beyond that, forget it.

As already mentioned, when my wife and I recently learned of multiple betrayals followed by the discovery that several people in our immediate circle had deceived us, it was crushing, heartbreaking and inwardly bloody. Talk about feeling like the rug has been pulled out from under you! This was more like the ground went with the rug.

Following the initial shock, we were, admittedly, dealing with very strong feelings toward the offenders. The people we thought were close friends had proven otherwise. It was like a walking, talking nightmare; a *Twilight Zone* episode written just for us. We wondered, *How is God letting them get away with this? Why doesn't He answer it? Where is He? How can He sit by and allow this to take place without responding on our behalf?* It appeared as if the heavens were brass. God seemed strangely silent. Very little in my entire Christian experience had ever tested my faith like this did.

I searched the Scriptures for answers to my pain, soaking up the stories of David, Job, Joseph and others who endured betrayal, deceit, giant setbacks and disappointments. I pored through Psalms, following David through field and cave, listening to his heartfelt prayers, his cries in the night and his grappling with the circumstances that had befallen him. I sat next to Job as he lay in the dirt, his skin covered with oozing sores, his faith hurled to the mat, his insensitive, tactless friends saying all the wrong things and his wife giving up on God in disgust. I wept with Joseph as he endured betrayal after betrayal, setback on top of setback and the shattering of all his dreams and hopes; a forgotten man in a stranger's land, but not forgotten by God.

Over time I began to see a pattern that had never occurred to me before. A repeated theme in these stories began to emerge. The message of God's sovereignty, the same message that I had touched on with Tony on the tennis courts, began to crystallize for me one morning when I read the following psalm: "Your path led through the sea, your way through the mighty waters, *though your footprints were not seen*" (Psalm 77:19, NIV, italics mine). The psalmist is remembering how God parted the waters for the children of Israel and miraculously led them across under Moses and Aaron. Allow me once again to turn to *The Message* to add a bit of punch to this verse: "From Whirlwind came your thundering voice, lightning exposed the world, earth reeled and rocked. You strode right through Ocean, walked straight through roaring Ocean, *but nobody saw you come or go*" (verses 18–19, italics mine).

Nobody saw you come or go. While reading those words on my back patio, the early morning sun rising slowly in the distance, something clicked in me that touched my heart with deep peace. It may seem simple, but for me it was an answer to my pain. *God is moving on our behalf all the time in ways we will never see or be aware of.* When I turned to Matthew Henry's commentary, I read these words:

> Though God is holy, just, and good, in all He does, yet we cannot give an account of the reasons of His proceedings, nor make any certain judgment of His designs. God's ways

are like the deep waters, which cannot be fathomed, like the way of a ship in the sea, which cannot be tracked.[4]

A liberating revelation began to dawn on me. *Providence leaves no footprints.* In other words, most of what God does in the earth is utterly unknown to the human eye. He is ever moving, ever orchestrating circumstances and people according to His grand design, and we never see it. *Nobody saw Him come or go.* Henry finally added, "God's proceedings are always to be acquiesced in, but cannot always be accounted for."[5]

When God says, "Vengeance is mine; I will repay" (Romans 12:19, KJV), you can count on three things: He will do what He said. It will not be executed in the *way* you would have done it. Nor will it happen *when* you would have done it. I realized that my ability to see or know what God was doing on our behalf was virtually nil. Joseph never saw the invisible steps of God marching him into Egypt, guiding his future and giving Pharaoh dreams only he could decipher. Only when the bigger picture emerged with Pharaoh crowning him second in charge of all Egypt did the pieces of the puzzle fall into place. David was only partially aware of God's silent hand at work for ten long years of wilderness wandering until, on what began as one of the worst days of his life, Saul was slain by the Philistines, and the crown came upon David's weary head in the perfect timing of God.

I have often wondered what became of Mrs. Potiphar, the deceiving wife of Potiphar, who had Joseph thrown into prison on a false accusation of sexual assault. We never hear of her again. Yet, God certainly answered what she had done to Joseph. Likewise, He will handle those who deceive and betray His children. As I mulled over the providence and sovereignty of God, it was so much easier to say in moments of discouragement, "I trust in the Lord, no matter how things look to my natural eye, for *He leaves no footprints.*"

I am convinced that the primary reason God tells us to leave vengeance to Him is to protect us from even further tragedy. Take a walk through any prison and you will see the sad consequences of taking personal vengeance in the faces of thousands of men and women. We are told not to do it because we would certainly mess it up, go too far, be unjust and ungodly in our response, and, most of all, it would not bring the healing we think it would. God says, "Leave it to Me," because only God sees the situation perfectly enough to divvy out the vengeance fairly.

The realization that God was leaving footprints of correction and discipline in places and hearts I would likely never know about freed me to focus on my own healing. My response, not the actions of others, would determine my future. Part of my crawling through the barbed wire of bitterness lay in the ability to release absolutely all consequences of others' actions to Him. Once I had trusted Him to handle my offenders, healing began in me.

This leads me to the final step in experiencing healing from a friendship turned painful: *Pray for your friend*. The book of Job tracks the life of one of the grandest characters in the ancient east. For reasons hard to understand, God permitted Satan to attack a thoroughly good man and to destroy everything he had but his life. Poor old Job is found sitting in a pile of ashes, his body covered in oozing sores, while his exasperated wife counseled him to "curse God and die!" (Job 2:9, NKJV).

As if he needed any more trouble, three of Job's "friends" arrived on the scene and proceeded to blame him for all that had taken place. The majority of the book focuses on the combative dialogue between Job and his well-meaning but ill-advised friends. In the closing chapter, God finally brought His much-needed verdict. "My wrath is aroused against you and your two friends, for you have not spoken of Me what is right," He thunderously exclaimed to Eliphaz (42:7, NKJV).

God then commanded the three men to approach Job in humility and allow him to pray for them. "And the LORD restored Job's losses when he prayed for his friends" (42:10, NKJV).

There is in Scripture a continual testimony to the connection between forgiveness and freedom, forgiveness and breakthrough, forgiveness and restoration. To forgive and pray for a friend who causes pain is to release the hand of God into that relationship.

Even when we have to crawl through the gnarly barbed wire of offense, He is faithful to provide a crawl space. In your experience with deception and betrayal, have you been able to embrace the truth that God longs to work this for your good? Can you see the incredible opportunity for spiritual growth? Are you currently entangled in the barbed wire of bitterness and looking for a way out? Choose forgiveness. Leave your offenders in the hands of God, pray for them and march into your future.

PART 3

LEAVERS

"Do you also want to leave?"
John 6:67

7

WHY LEAVERS LEAVE

Most people around here are looking out for themselves.

Philippians 2:21

Friendships can die for a variety of reasons; some major, and others from simple wear and tear over a period of time. Neglect, change or betrayal can do the trick. Starting a romance, getting married or having kids has also been known to end many a friendship. Drs. Les and Leslie Parrott point out that friendship can end with a bang or a whimper. "Those that whimper simply dissolve from neglect, having run their natural course. They quietly cross some threshold, and the break comes to pass without much fanfare."

But friendships that end with a bang do so for more compelling reasons. It is "more likely the result of an un-expected change or a more dreadful betrayal. You amass enough incremental bitterness (or it comes in one lump sum) and you have one too many unsatisfying encounters, then one of you erupts."[1]

My friend Jackie met the man she would ultimately marry and was, naturally, very excited. Jackie is a wonderful lady with a quiet spirit and a beautiful singing voice. I was very happy for her and was honored to play a part in the ceremony. One night after she and Bill were married, they invited me (I was still single) over for dinner. The three of us had a great time kicked back on their couch in the living room talking, just letting the night slip by. During the course of conversation, Bill suddenly said something to Jackie in front of me that was very disrespectful and embarrassing to both of us. It was a criticism at her expense. I tried jumping in and changing the subject, but what had taken place lingered in the room like something palpable.

As I drove away that night, I knew deep down that, much as I hated it, their marriage was in trouble. Now mind you, I was no relationship expert and had not yet been married myself. This was one of those moments that do not come real often when God's Spirit decides to minister a truth to you about something. In this case He seemed to be saying, "Jeff, respect is foundational to any successful relationship, friendship or otherwise. When respect leaves, it's over." I knew that, though they had only been married less than a year, the seeds of failure were already present.

Years later I received a desperate, anguished call. It was Jackie. Bill had left her and was also in trouble with the law. Left with two children and little earning capacity, she was heartbroken and shattered. I, however, was not surprised. What did surprise me was that it had taken so long. And I also was not surprised at her response when I volunteered to talk to him. "No!" she said emphatically. "I'd rather be alone than be treated this way."

While Bill and Jackie's was a marital experience, the same principle holds true for friendships. There must be a mutual respect, or the disrespected one will eventually leave in search of the affirmation he or she deserves. Rome's greatest orator, Cicero, concurs. "Remove respect from friendship and you have taken away the most splendid ornament it possesses."[2]

I have never seen this principle of respect fail to prove true. Friendship is both strong and fragile. No contract holds it together. No family depends on its survival. While it can withstand great storms from without, it is delicate within, requiring both nurturing and mutual respect.

There are both good reasons and bad for leaving a relationship. Sometimes it is the healthiest thing you can do, as when respect is gone and you are being devalued. And often it is a natural evolution out of something that has grown apart with neither party objecting. But there are also times when leaving is a cop-out, when you are bailing out for all the wrong reasons.

But before we delve further into the subject of leaving, I would like to draw a distinction between leavers (those who leave a friendship) and deceivers (those who stick around, but whose hearts are gone). Deceivers stand in stark contrast to someone who, for a variety of reasons, reaches a breaking point in a relationship and chooses to walk away. His or her actions are very different from the deceiver who, rather than deal with a faltering relationship honestly and openly, chooses, for whatever reason, to play both sides of the fence. Deceivers walk away in their hearts while still standing by your side. They are users. Remember Judas? The Judas type possesses an uncanny, almost chilling ability to compartmentalize relationships, to have you "over here" while someone else may be "over there." In other words, theirs is a divided heart. In high school we called them "two-faced."

On the other hand, the kind of leaver we are focusing on in this chapter is not duplicitous. No ulterior motives keep them hanging around to "have their cake and eat it, too." Once the breaking point is reached, they hit the door. But, as we will see, not always for the best of reasons.

For example, you probably know the Old Testament story of Ruth. The curtain rises on a man named Elimelech, his wife, Naomi, and their two sons. When a famine strikes their hometown of Bethlehem, they flee, eventually pitching their tent in the land of Moab. Sadly, Elimelech soon dies. In the meantime the two boys marry local girls, Orpah and Ruth. As the story progresses, the two boys also eventually die, leaving three heartbroken widows to fend for themselves.

Beside herself with grief, Naomi begins urging her two daughters-in-law to return to their people, for they were both Moabites. In the story, both women initially declare their undying allegiance to their bereaved mother-in-law. "And they said to her, 'Surely we will return with you to your people'" (Ruth 1:10, NKJV). But things soon change. On further reflection, Orpah decides it is time to go. Following her departure, Naomi's words to Ruth reveal that Orpah had at least been honest about why she was leaving: "'Look,' Naomi said to her, 'your sister-in-law has gone back to her people and to her gods'" (Ruth 1:15, NLT).

Orpah's had been a clean, honest break. No game playing, no stringing Naomi along, just "I want to go home. I miss my family and my religion."

The Bottom Line

The whole issue of leavers and deceivers boils down to one question: Which is better—a lie that draws a smile, or the truth that draws a tear? Which would you prefer? Painful as the truth may sometimes be, in most cases you and I would rather be told the truth than to discover we were lied to, strung along in someone else's game.

It seems to me that ours has become a "leaving" culture. As a pastor, I cannot tell you how often my ministry brethren have poured their hearts out in frustration over the revolving back door in their churches. "I have no idea why they leave," one pastor lamented to me. "They seem happy, and are often deeply involved with the church. No known problem exists that I know anything about, and suddenly, without warning, they just up and leave without even saying good-bye—after years of relationship!" Another pastor at a ministers' conference painfully described how family after family had left his church until, one afternoon following a phone call from yet another departing family, his wife fell to the floor weeping her eyes out, unable to any longer make sense of the "leaving" mentality among God's people.

The same phenomenon is true for Christian marriages. "Born again Christians are just as likely to get divorced as are non-born again adults," reports a recent George Barna poll.[3] "Overall, 33 percent of all born again individuals who have been married have gone through a divorce, which is statistically identical to the 34 percent incidence among non-born again adults."[4]

"I've Had All I Can Stands!"

You may recall the famous cartoon character Popeye from the '60s and '70s. If not, I have just dated myself. I used to make a beeline home each afternoon after school to catch *Popeye*, along with, of course, *Superman*. That one-hour time block was the highlight of my day. Popeye, the sailor man, was an easygoing guy with a happy-go-lucky, upbeat attitude toward life. His girlfriend, Olive Oyl, seemed to have a knack for getting in trouble with bullies, the king of which was a brute named Brutus.

In virtually every program, Popeye wound up getting pushed to the brink—usually over Olive Oyl being rudely hit on by Brutus—at which time he would produce a can of spinach, which he proceeded to inhale in one gulp. Immediately his forearms would swell to huge proportions and the sailor man would be endowed with near supernatural strength. No foe could withstand his lightning-fast,

121

powerful strike. He always won the day, the girl and my young-boy admiration.

Popeye had a saying that preceded every decision to consume the spinach and whip the villain at hand. You knew that feathers were about to fly when he belted out, "I've had all I can stands; I can't stands no more!" His lack of good grammar aside, there was something refreshing about that statement. "I've had all I can stands; I can't stands no more!"

We all reach breaking points, those defining moments when we have had "all we can stands" and, by golly, "we can't stands no more!" Action must be taken; something has to change. Yet, increasingly, the answer of choice is to exit, which, unfortunately, can short-circuit valuable lessons that could be learned. To reach all you can stand is not necessarily the signal moment to exit. It may be the nudge to dig deep and learn some of the keys to sustaining a relationship.

I do not pretend to understand all the reasons why there seems to be such an issue with people leaving their commitments in our day. I only know what I have observed as someone who has worked with others a great deal. Aside from the general friendship-enders like moving, marriage, newfound faith or a natural drifting apart through changing interests, let's explore a few of the deadly friendship busters.

That's Enough about Me, Now Let's Talk about Me

We live in a selfish culture. In fact, it is a war zone. The false messages invading our Western minds are like bombs incessantly dropping out of a dark and sinister sky. "You deserve the best. Go for the gusto. Get all you can out of life. He who dies with the most toys wins. If it feels good, do it. Take care of number one. It is all about you and

your personal fulfillment!" Of course, all of these philosophical sound bites are utterly unbiblical. Yet they have
wormed their way into the subconscious of our generation
and polluted its soul. *It is all about us.* Paul the apostle put
it in a nutshell: "Most people around here are looking out
for themselves, with little concern for the things of Jesus"
(Philippians 2:21).

That nails a big part of the problem. When people believe that it is all about them—looking out for themselves,
making themselves happy, acquiring things for themselves—you have a recipe for disaster in a relationship.
A friendship is all about sharing, giving and sacrificing
for the other. It is give and take, bend and bow, flex and
flow. When selfish people are required to stretch, forgive
or sacrifice, when their style is cramped and they become
inconvenienced, they will leave in search of less demanding
pastures.

For instance, take the church shopping issue. Even in
our church hunting, it is all about us. "What is this church
going to do for *me*?" "Will they meet *my* needs?" we wonder.
"I expect this, and this, and this and, oh, this, too," has become our mantra. It may surprise you to know that the New
Testament suggests quite a different motive for involvement
in a church body. "Each one should use whatever gift he
has received to serve others, faithfully administering God's
grace in its various forms" (1 Peter 4:10, NIV).

Catch that, for it changed my entire view of church.
God has given every single Christian on earth a gift for the
purpose of serving others.

Blessing others through servanthood is the message of this
verse. And it is exactly this attitude that enriches a friendship.
Imagine entering a new friendship with the primary question
being, "What does God want me to *give* in this relationship?
What can I offer to help this person?" Next time the feeling
to flee a relationship arises, ask yourself, "Is this really the
time to leave, or is it an opportunity to change or serve?"

Believe me when I tell you, when God decides to chisel away your selfishness, it will never be pleasant, but the end result is worth it. Friendships can be His tool of choice.

The Need Only God Can Touch

In chapter 12 I discuss the ultimate friendship—friendship with God—because without it we will all live lives of frustration. We all sometimes look to people to fulfill a level of need that only God can. There is in each of our souls a God-shaped hole, and no human being on earth is equipped to fulfill that longing—only He is. We are aware of a hunger deep inside, but we do not accurately read it. So we go in search of that one magic relationship that will satiate it, and we wind up frustrated every time. The poor people we drag into our lives with the expectation that they will meet that need never quite pull it off. So, in frustration, we leave. And leave. And leave; ever in search of the right fix. I have done it. We all have.

The solution starts with understanding, as I have already mentioned, that we are broken creatures. Something is broken in all of us. In the Garden of Eden our life-flow from God was unplugged as a result of sin. Designed to live and move and have our being in Him, without Christ we are now adrift in a world that was designed for us to enjoy exclusively in relationship with our Maker.

There is no question in my mind that this is what people are looking for in substance abuse: the peace, euphoria and sense of well-being that finds its righteous fulfillment only in fellowship with God through Jesus Christ. Until we allow Him to fulfill the longing that only He can, we humans will live with a dull ache, an inexplicable loneliness, a frustrating itch we just cannot seem to scratch. Next time you decide to exit a relationship, ask yourself, "Is it possible I'm looking to this relationship to do for me what only God can?"

Too Much Nice

Contrary to what many think, Jesus did not teach His followers to be nice. He did, however, teach us to walk in love. Christians are too nice. There, I said it. How, you may ask, can being nice kill a friendship? Nice can kill a friendship because it keeps us from being honest with each other about our feelings. Moses gave us the Ten Commandments, but Jesus only gave one. "Let me give you a new command: Love one another. In the same way I loved you, you love one another" (John 13:34).

Jesus commanded us to love each other *in the same way* He loved us. When I think of just how Jesus loved His disciples, I can lift some examples from Scripture when Christ was not nice but was indeed loving. For instance, following Jesus' declaration to His disciples that He must go to Jerusalem, suffer many things from the elders, chief priests and scribes and ultimately be killed, a distraught Simon Peter "took Him aside and began to rebuke Him, saying, 'Far be it from You, Lord; this shall not happen to You!'" (Matthew 16:22, NKJV).

Now, the *nice* thing would have been for Jesus to wrap an arm around Peter and say, "Now, now, Peter. I know all this talk about My death is very upsetting to you, but we're going to make it through this. I promise!" Instead, Jesus turned around in a flash and said, "Get behind me, Satan! You are a stumbling block to me; you do not have in mind the things of God, but the things of men" (verse 23, NIV). Nice? No. Loving? Yes! Peter's deepest need was to know the truth that he was, at that point in time, not thinking about the good of the Kingdom of God, but of his own selfish wishes.

Political correctness has invaded the Church, and it is scary. Our concept of Christian living has evolved into the idea that to say something painfully truthful is not "walking in love." So instead we are *nice*. Webster's defines *nice* as, "pleasant, agreeable."[5] There have been times when I wanted to say, "Quit being so nice, and get real!" To me, too nice is like too much chocolate. If it is not mixed with genuineness it can make you sick. For a friendship to survive, there must be times of openness and honesty when the lid comes off and what is inside comes out.

We are afraid that if we are truthful, it will destroy the friendship. And you know what? It might. But things can reach a point where it is destroyed anyway if you do not get honest. Marla Paul in her book, *The Friendship Crisis*, points out, "We expect to spar with a spouse, or a boyfriend or girlfriend. The bonds of a romance or marriage yank us back to repair the damage. Friendships, however, are bound only by the pleasure in each other's company. We're afraid they're assembled from glass—and not the shatterproof kind."[6]

Don't get me wrong. I am certainly not advocating being abrasive, tactless, impolite or cruel. I *am* advocating genuineness and transparency, the courage to be real. If you do not practice this, the large and small irritations, misunderstandings, unmet needs and disappointments that arise in any friendship are going to chip away at it till nothing is left. One day one of you will wake up and think, *I've had all I can stands*. "Having the moxie to unveil your non-warm and non-fuzzy feelings can actually save a friendship."[7] So, the next time you decide to leave a relationship, be honest with yourself; is it because you have pent-up feelings you have not had the courage to talk about? Try talking. You may find that it unstops the dam and allows the warmth of friendship to flow again.

The Green-Eyed Dragon

Nobody likes to admit to jealousy. It is humiliating at best to tell people that you hate their guts because they are so blasted good at what they do, have achieved a particular level of success or look like they just stepped off of a magazine cover. Envy and jealousy are used interchangeably in Scripture with just a wee bit of distinction. Envy wants what someone else has, like a nice house, great job, hot car, hot boyfriend or girlfriend, etc. Jealousy is the tormenting feeling over their having it. Envy says, "I want it." Jealousy says, "Drat, they have it!" Jealousy and envy can slaughter a friendship.

For me, the most tormenting emotion in human experience has got to be jealousy, even more than fear. Solomon observed, "We're blasted by anger and swamped by rage, but who can survive jealousy?" (Proverbs 27:4). The Hebrew description of *jealousy* is "that which causes color in the face by deep emotion."[8] The Song of Solomon describes jealousy as being "hard and cruel as Sheol (the place of the dead). Its flashes are flashes of fire, a most vehement flame" (Song of Solomon 8:6, AMPLIFIED).

If you want to connect an IV drip of strychnine to a friendship, just let jealousy through the door. When I was a kid— around seven or eight years old—I had a friend on my block named Johnny. Though he was a couple of years older than me, we were buds. We did all the regular guy stuff together like playing marbles, riding bikes, playing catch and just hanging out. The first time I can remember experiencing the hot stab of jealousy was the day I realized my dad got along with Johnny, too. In fact, he would even walk down the street to say hi to him and chat a bit. The green-eyed monster began to growl deep in my heart. To make matters even worse, he would come home and tell my mom something funny Johnny had said, bragging on his wit.

The clincher took place when my dad burst in the door one evening to announce that Johnny could sure hit a heck of a good golf shot! "Really?" my mom asked. "How do you know?"

"Because we walked across the street to the field, and he drove it out of sight!"

Remember that description of "color in the face"? The red flush of hurt and anger rushed into my countenance. Surprising even myself, I blurted, "Then why don't you just be Johnny's best friend!" My dad's face had that deer-staring-at-headlights expression. Jealousy had gotten the best of me and, yes, it ruined my friendship with Johnny.

Sometimes I have felt that I would have better luck escaping an army of angry bees than shaking the stinging emotion of jealousy. Socrates once advised that a man should marry; if he got a good wife, he would become happy; if not, the wise choice would be to become a philosopher. That has proven good advice for me as it relates to working through situations that have produced jealousy. I try to look at it from a philosophical angle, in such a way that it pulls the stinger out. If I can find purpose in something, I can handle almost anything. When experiencing the miserable torment of jealousy, try repeating a few of the following statements to yourself:

- *Unlike us, God's love does not want what it does not have.* "Love never is envious nor boils over with jealousy" (1 Corinthians 13:4, AMPLIFIED). Tell yourself that this is an excellent opportunity to learn to walk in the freedom real love brings.
- *I won't always feel this way.* This, too, shall pass. Circumstances, surroundings and people will change.
- *God's plan for me is as wonderful as is His plan for someone else.* What is happening in someone else's life is no reflection of what is happening in yours.
- *God is in control of my life.* What He wants you to have, you will have. What He does not want you to have, you do not want anyway. Trust God!

If jealousy is threatening a relationship, ask yourself if it is valid. Try rejoicing in your friend's success. One sure way to gain the upper hand is to verbally congratulate him or her. If someone compliments him or her in front of you, agree and throw in your own two cents. This has a way of disarming jealousy's destructive emotions.

Unresolved Issues

Some issues in life—like taxes and relationship conflicts—will not get out of your face. If you cannot ignore them, you had better negotiate with them. That is good advice for anyone wanting to keep a friendship. Learn to talk through issues that bring conflict, and do not sit on it too long. *Offended hearts only grow harder the longer you wait.*

Whatever your issues are—jealousy, misunderstanding, some petty thing that got blown out of proportion—it is up to you whether they are going to kill your friendship. Someone has to make the first move, so it might as well be you. Jesus taught us how to handle breaches in relationships, something I wrote about extensively in my book *Making It Right When You Feel Wronged.* Allow me to briefly revisit some of what I said. Read thoughtfully Jesus' instructions on handling offenses. For the sake of staying true to the friendship theme of this book, let's replace *brother* with *friend.*

> If your [friend] wrongs you, go and show him his fault, between you and him privately. If he listens to you, you have won back your [friend].
>
> Matthew 18:15, AMPLIFIED

So, "If a *friend* sins against you . . ." *Sin* comes from a Greek word meaning "to miss the mark."[9] Something was said, done or not done that just totally missed your need as a friend. Rather than being there, understanding, reaching out, being more sensitive or supporting you, your friend dropped the ball. One of two things happened as a result: It caused a very unpleasant fight or launched a cold war. You are refusing his or her calls, or vice versa. Maybe nobody is calling at all. Now there is a breach.

This happened with my fireman friend, Frank, and me over a stupid racquetball game. Guys are hopelessly competitive creatures. We can praise the Lord and shout hallelujah like spiritual giants until we enter a contest against each other. Then it is dog-eat-dog, go-for-the-jugular, cutthroat competition. On this particular day, Frank and I had a disagreement over rules in the middle of the game. It happened not once, not twice, but several times. I finally got so mad I stormed out of the court and headed straight for the front desk to ask for a rule book. They did not have one, so I presented my cosmically important case to one of the employees, who quickly sized up the situation and figured he was stepping into the middle of a land mine. By now Frank had walked up, and we stood there waiting for the guy's verdict like the fate of the United States depended on it. Wisely, the poor guy said he did not know.

For days Frank and I did not talk. Finally, I knew what must be done. We met and faced it. "I acted like an idiot, Frank," I told him, knowing it was true. "Well, Pastor, I didn't mean to argue. It was stupid. Forgive me," Frank said in a low, humble voice. Immediately the tension lifted. We have played some good games since then. But you know what? That one stupid game could have distanced us forever had our pride allowed it!

Jesus suggested a thirteen-letter word most of us do not like: *confrontation*. In other words, do not allow a breach to simmer for too long. Do something. Make a move. Act. Save the relationship if you can before someone leaves. Jesus said, "Go and show him his fault, between you and him privately." Successful confrontation is not easy. We need wisdom. Consider some of the following pointers:

- *Pray before you go.* Strike when the iron is cold, after you have had time to cool down. You may realize that it is not as big a deal as you thought at first.
- *Examine yourself.* Is your reaction equal to the event, or is it off the charts? Could other issues be at play? Are you under stress at work? Home? With the kids? You may be projecting some of your frustration onto your friend. "Why do you look at the speck of sawdust in your brother's eye and pay no attention to the plank in your own eye?" (Matthew 7:3, NIV).
- *Choose your wording carefully.* "The heart of the godly thinks carefully before speaking; the mouth of the wicked overflows with evil words" (Proverbs 15:28, NLT). Try not to use accusing language. Do not interrupt. Above all, keep the decibel level down. "A gentle response defuses anger, but a sharp tongue kindles a temper-fire" (Proverbs 15:1).
- *Be a good listener.* James advises, "Understand this, my dear brothers and sisters: You must all be quick to listen, slow to speak, and slow to get angry" (James 1:19, NLT). Remember, this is a give-and-take proposition. Listen carefully to what your friend says. Keep the goal in mind—you are saving a valuable friendship. "If he listens to you, you have won your brother over" (Matthew 18:15, NIV).

In this chapter we have learned that there is a fundamental difference between leavers and deceivers. And we have examined some of the reasons why leavers leave, some good and some ill-advised. In the next chapter we will explore a few more of the reasons why some people hit the trail, never to be seen again.

8

ANGELS IN DISGUISE

> Some people have welcomed angels without knowing it.
>
> Hebrews 13:2, NIrV

Many years ago, at the age of thirteen, I had a best friend named Joe. Joe's father was an alcoholic and basically wreaked havoc on his entire household with his out-of-control temper and violence. One unforgettable time, I went on vacation with Joe's family. We drove somewhere far away, I do not remember where, but I do remember the hellacious drive. His dad threw back one beer after another all the way there, passing in no-passing lanes, shouting at his protesting wife and generally terrifying all of us. Joe, I recall, was enormously embarrassed for me to catch this glimpse into his private life. He could not look me in the eye, nor could he put on his "I'm cool" facade.

Burned in my memory is our arrival at the hotel late that night. Intensely relieved to be out of the car, I took a few steps into the parking lot just in time for Joe to get out and scream at the top of his lungs, "Why can't we be happy!" He then burst into tears, unable to give a whit any longer whether I saw the truth of his life. That pain, so deep, so total, is the pain that, I am convinced, brought Joe to the place where I buried him at 51 years of age—the broken product of a lifetime of trying to medicate himself into a numb stupor with drugs, alcohol, anything and everything.

My history with Joe went something like this. After I gave my heart to Christ when still a teenager, Joe pooh-poohed my decision and predicted my return to a life of substance abuse and partying. That never happened, and we lost touch for over two decades. I went into the ministry, and Joe continued down his self-destructive path. One night at around two in the morning, I received a phone call from his ex-wife. She informed me that my former friend was holed up in a fleabag hotel and was threatening suicide. "Will you go talk to him?" she asked in desperation. Talk about a blast from the past. Pulling on my jeans and a T-shirt, I drove in the dead of night down seedy streets filled with seedy-looking people, thinking back to the last time I had seen him. He had lit a joint in front of me and blown it into my face. "You'll be back, Jeff."

Walking down the dingy, "no-tell motel" corridor looking for his room number, I was wondering if I should have brought a weapon. Sinister-looking people were checking out my car and me. When I knocked on the door, a voice yelled, "Who is it?" "Jeff Wickwire, Joe," I said as firmly as I knew how. The door slowly opened, revealing a smoke-filled rat's nest. He was as shocked to see me as I was to see him. The suicide concoction was on the night table, just as Jane had told me, ready to guzzle. The Joe I had once known was not the Joe I saw before me. His once handsome face was worn and tired. Deep, dark bags shadowed his bloodshot eyes. Quite unlike the fit, athletic guy I remembered, he was overweight, the result of cheap food and sedentary living.

I talked him out of his plan to end it all that night. And in the next few years I did my level best to get him on his feet. We went to a couple of concerts for old time's sake, anything to reintroduce him to the land of the living. And I got him checked into rehab. But time and again he would relapse into his self-destructive lifestyle. I will be honest. After a few of the relapses and more rehabs, I found myself saying, "What is this? Why am I here? I'm giving so much time to him, and he keeps going back!" When I took all of this to God in prayer, that still small voice of the Holy Spirit seemed to say, *Just love him.*

Joe also had a son from his former marriage who was dying from muscular dystrophy. This was, naturally, ripping his heart out. Everything that Joe had possessed—a successful contracting business, beautiful wife, great house, lots of friends—was now gone. Drugs had reduced him to sleeping in a halfway house with a little box containing all his belongings. When his son died, I went to the funeral. After the heartrending slide show of the brief life Kirk had known, I had a feeling, just a feeling, that the little bit Joe had to live for was now gone. But God seemed to keep saying, *Love him. Forgive his failings and just love him.*

The call came one morning from the director of his halfway house. Joe had been found dead in his bed, apparently the result of continued drug abuse. His body just could not take it anymore. I think he finally just gave up the fight. His former wife asked me to break the news to his daughter, who was on her way to town with some clothes and stuff for Joe. It was one of the hardest things I have ever had to do. Joe's funeral, though very sad, was not quite as difficult. Held at the graveside, the weather matched the way I felt. It was cold, overcast and raining, sending a chill to my bones. Had it really come to this? My friend, whose cry for help I had heard at thirteen, who had left my life for so long only to return toward the end, had been cremated.

His remains rested in a little urn directly in front of me as I spoke to those gathered.

Driving home that day, I rehearsed all that had taken place those last few years between Joe and me; the times I got frustrated and wanted to walk away; the words God had spoken to me about loving him; the times I went and picked him up for a simple drive or to go to lunch; the times I had muttered, "What is this all for?" And it occurred to me that they had been as much for me as they had been for him. Joe, for certain, was not what I would have prayed to come into my life in the way that he had. He did not look like a blessing at the time. He drew a question mark rather than an exclamation point. Yet, as I stayed, forgave him, put on patience and took him to yet another halfway house after yet another failure, a little bit of Christlikeness was chiseled into my soul. And Joe? I like to think that he died having experienced someone treating him like Jesus would have.

This all brings me to a topic you will think is very much unrelated—*friendship and manna*. Let me explain. God often visits our everyday lives via blessings in disguise. He does not always tell us what He is up to and, in essence, approaches by stealth. Though His primary way of speaking to us is through His Word, it is not His *only* way. Some of the people addressed in the book of Hebrews, for instance, had actually been visited by angels without their knowing it. The writer admonishes, "Do not forget to entertain strangers, for by so doing some people have entertained angels without knowing it" (Hebrews 13:2, NIV). And this brings me to the children of Israel and this manna thing.

Manna Issues

God's freshly delivered people had just begun their journey through the wilderness when He decided to feed them

with what they chose to call *manna*. The Hebrew meaning
for manna is "What is it?"[1] "When the Israelites first saw
the manna lying there like dew on the ground, they looked
at each other and asked the logical question, 'What is it?'"[2]
Hence, the name.

There was no precedent for manna, nothing Israel could
access in some file somewhere in order to learn more about
it. It was a brand-new, first-time, never-seen-before substance, like Silly Putty or Big Macs once were. Manna came
in the form of small, round seed that resembled frost on
the ground. Every morning, the Almighty faithfully deposited "what is it" on the ground for them to gather. If not
collected early before the sun rose, it melted. And it had
zero preservatives. If not consumed that day, it became
wormy and rotted. It was prepared for eating by grinding
and then baking it. And manna really did not taste bad.
"Manna tasted like fresh oil, like wafers made with honey,
equally agreeable to all palates."[3]

Now, I will be the first to admit that *anything* would get
old after a few years, not to mention forty years. Eventually,
they began to despise their daily manna. But—and this is
what I want you to catch—there was more behind the manna
in terms of God's purposes than simply food to eat, and this
is what Israel missed, as we can with relationships.

In Psalm 78 the writer, Asaph, calls manna "angels' food"
and the "bread of heaven." "Men ate angels' food," claims
Asaph; "He sent them food to the full" (Psalm 78:25, NKJV).

Whether Asaph meant that manna was the actual food on
which angels subsisted or food supplied by the ministration
of angels is not the point. What Israel failed to discern were
the lessons God was trying to teach them through the manna.
Remember something very important: *Anything* God brings
into our lives is designed to develop character, to further
conform us into the image of His Son. He is always working
in us to bring that high purpose to pass. Remember that "all
things" issue we talked about in chapter 5?

137

It is no mistake that Scripture calls manna "the bread of the mighty angels" (Psalm 78:24). While its primary use was for food, character-developing lessons lay behind it that could have played a key role in Israel's future, better preparing them for the Promised Land.

Speaking of which, I have learned that God sometimes brings people into my life who are just like manna: If I open my eyes, I can see that they are there to teach me. *They* are not the actual teachers, but my interactions with them are. People can, in a sense, arrive as manna in disguise. For instance, have you ever looked at a longtime friend and said to yourself, "This is getting old. I want a change!"? But whoever said that all of God's blessings were at all times pleasurable? Many of God's blessings arrive clothed in difficulty but with perseverance wind up blossoming into joy.

Let's carry this one step further and compare what Israel learned from their manna to what we can learn through the ups and downs of friendship. Three key lessons were presented to them via manna: *humility, thanksgiving* and *trust*. Let's explore them.

First, the manna was *humbling*. Has a friendship ever really humbled you? For instance, when you blew it and offended your friend and needed to ask forgiveness? Or, when that friendship revealed things about you that were humbling and needed to change, like my lack of patience with Joe? Israel had needed desperately to learn the lesson of humility and missed it by badly responding to the manna. It is mind-boggling to read of their brazen arrogance and stubbornness before the God who had led them with a cloud by day and a blazing fire by night, had made water gush from a rock and had delivered them from the chains of Egypt.

> How often in the desert they had spurned him, tried his patience in those wilderness years. Time and again they pushed him to the limit, provoked Israel's Holy God.
>
> Psalm 78:40–41

The manna was designed not just to feed them but also to *change* them. *Psst, so are friendships*. If they would have been better off with daily quail, which we will see in a moment they demanded from God, they would have had *had* daily quail. But walking out of their tents at the break of day in order to gather "what is it" was humbling, and they did not like that. There was nothing extravagant about breakfast in the wilderness. This was not IHOP. They had either baked, fried, broiled or raw manna. No one said, "What's for breakfast?" They knew the answer . . . *manna.* And for forty years!

Second, the manna was designed to make them *thankful.* I believe one of the great keys to successful relationships is the ability to be thankful. If all you see are your friend's faults, that friendship is headed for the rocks. Israel had to be one of the most unthankful bunches of people in history. Their tongues literally became shovels by which they dug their own graves. Listen to just one of the descriptions of their ungratefulness and its consequences. "Now these things are examples (warnings and admonitions) for us not to . . . discontentedly complain as some of them did—and were put out of the way entirely by the destroyer (death)" (1 Corinthians 10:6, 10, AMPLIFIED).

Think about that a moment. Complaining literally killed them! "Who will give us meat to eat? We remember the fish which we ate freely in Egypt, the cucumbers, the melons, the leeks, the onions, and the garlic; but now . . . there is nothing at all except this manna before our eyes!" (Numbers 11:4–6, NKJV). One thing is certain: The day you complain more than you thank is the day you need to stuff your mouth with a sock. When considering Israel's attitude, I remember once hearing a country preacher say, "Whatever you do, don't tick God off." Finally, Israel ticked God off. They continued to murmur aloud: "Sure, he struck the rock and the water flowed, creeks cascaded from the rock. But how about some fresh-baked bread? How about a nice cut of meat?" (Psalm 78:20). That did it. God finally said, "You want meat? I'll give you meat!"

> He let East Wind break loose from the skies, gave a strong push to South Wind. This time it was birds that rained down—succulent birds, an abundance of birds. He aimed them right for the center of their camp; all round their tents there were birds. They ate and had their fill; he handed them everything they craved on a platter.
>
> verses 26–29

This was unreal! Succulent quail dropping out of heaven like rain. I can almost hear them laughing with glee as the coveted birds fell at their feet, first-class room service from the Almighty. Scripture says they dug in with gusto. "But their greed knew no bounds; they stuffed their mouths with more and more" (verse 30).

They say that if it is too good to be true, it probably is. It sure was in this case. You see, God finally gave them what they wanted. But they sure did not want what they got once they got it, because it was not God's best. "And He gave them their request, but sent leanness into their souls" (Psalm 106:15, AMPLIFIED).

I point out this quail story because we can do this very same thing with a friend. Through selfishness and lack of a grateful heart, we may wind up rejecting a God-given opportunity to learn humility, thanksgiving and trust, in order to replace a friend with "quail." Quail friends are typically the popular, successful and good-looking; the power brokers of our social circle whose friendship will grant us greater status and esteem. I am talking about the age-old practice of sucking up to enhance our social standing at the expense of a friend.

One day while flipping through my Bible, I spotted a Scripture that has jumped back into my head on more than one occasion that talks about this very thing. "Don't be stuck-up. Make friends with nobodies; don't be the great somebody" (Romans 12:16). Paul's words shoot an arrow straight through the heart of the practice of what we might politely call "posterior kissing." We are not to try to be "the great somebody," says Paul, but rather should *on purpose* befriend nobodies! I have a friend who recently told me of a very wealthy man he knows, who purposefully visits the homeless under bridges and on the streets. He gives them food and talks to them. He says he does it to keep himself grounded. Good and true friends keep us grounded.

Quail friends usually are not all you expected anyway. In fact, when you go for quail, you usually get burned, just like Israel did. "But before they turned from the food they craved, even while it was still in their mouths, God's anger rose against them" (Psalm 78:30–31, NIV). Quail friends tend to be very shallow, self-serving people who seem to be at a loss when it comes to meaningful friendships, which is another reason leavers jump ship—they simply cannot handle intimacy.

It is not that God gets angry when we resort to posterior kissing for political purposes, but I do believe He gets grieved, because pride is at the core of it. I think this is one of the reasons I am not a big preachers' conference person. It is not that I do not like preachers; I do. It is that when I have attended some of these conferences (not all), a whole lot of posterior kissing to the preachers with the bigger churches has gone on. I have seen more business cards exchanged at a pastors' conference than baseball cards at a card convention. And it is always with the promise, "Hey, fantastic! I'll give you a call and we'll fellowship some!" These usually prove to be vacuous words with no follow-up at all. Of course, I am not the greatest caller either, but I also do not pass out many business cards.

Humility, gratefulness and trust are learned through the small stuff in life, the manna stuff, like friendships. Later on, all of that transfers to the big stuff: Promised Land

141

stuff. Look around you as you read these words. Got any "manna" type friends in your orbit? I urge you to look beyond what you see with your natural eye and ask God what He is trying to teach you with them. It may just be that you are looking at manna from heaven, an angel in disguise, God's hammer and chisel in the form of a friend.

I now know that this is what Joe was for me. In staying with him, refusing to walk away when God said "stay," a little bit more of Christ was chiseled out in me, which is what I truly want. In a way, he was a gift sent in the disguise of a problem.

As with the Israelites, often it is all about us and not about what God may be trying to teach us. Despite the progress of our modern age—perhaps because of it—we are, in this way, very much like the Israelites. In our increasingly fast-paced, noncommittal world, we tend to avoid "manna" friendships that require forgiveness, sacrifice, loyalty and long-suffering, the things that stretch our faith and chisel out character.

Revolutions

Over one hundred years ago, you and I may have met fifteen new people in a year. Sounds absurd, right? Before the Industrial Revolution of the late eighteenth century transformed the American landscape, most people grew up on farms. Life revolved around the home. There was no television to distract us from each other, no cars to carry us miles and hours from home at the turn of a key. You probably would have attended a little country church somewhere close by, where everyone knew everyone else. The friends you would have made were likely people from your neck of the woods, who would have remained your friends throughout much of your life. After all, who else was around? The slower paced and close-knit communities of this agrarian lifestyle contributed to stronger, deeper relationships. Because of the close proximity, one was forced to work *through* relationship issues rather than just moving on.

All of that has dramatically changed. In addition to the Industrial Revolution, we have now experienced the technological revolution, and are currently speeding down the information superhighway of the *communications revolution*. We have come a very long way from the days of encountering around fifteen new people a year while living in a simple farming community. Global communication via the personal computer and the World Wide Web has launched communication into the stratosphere.

Not too awfully long ago, the Internet was used mainly for communications between government agencies and academics. No more. This new means of communication has opened up, true to its name, a *world*. People now have a *cyber life*. Electronic mail (email) has paved the way to communicate with others around the world at the click of a mouse button, and, happily, free of charge. Utilizing a simple chat program, you and I can now talk live to someone in Shanghai, China, whenever we like, to our heart's content, at no cost.

And talk about a revolution! According to the latest Center for Media Research report, in eleven short years, online use has jumped from 9 to 77 percent![4] Personal home computer and Internet use among Americans has leaped off the charts. Computers have taken over in a mere nanosecond.

Now, how many encounters with new people do you suppose this new communications medium has produced? Before you answer, be sure you add to the personal computer the popular Blackberry, the Sidekick (also known as Hiptop, a mobile service and device that offers integrated phone, HTML web-browsing, email, instant messaging and other entertainment features), iPods, laptops and the ever-present cell phone. Speaking of which, just the other night I was speaking to a crowd of around one thousand people in a church setting. Before introducing me, the host requested that the lights be dimmed, then asked everyone to get out their cell phones, open the faces and hold them up. Virtually everyone had one, and instead of lighting the room with candles, we lit it with cell phones! What a sight to see a thousand cell phones waved in the dark. Times have changed.

This deluge of communication has even brought about the coining of a new word—*friendini*. What is a friendini? A friendini is a friend who is there one minute and, like a Houdini, disappears in the next. Poof! Now you see him, now you don't. It is just another phrase for friendship-lite, low-cal relationship, diet dalliances, sugar-free commitment. Tastes great, but definitely less filling.

In a recent segment on the television program *Showbiz Tonight*, the connection between technology and loneliness was the hot topic. Dr. Gail Saltz, a psychiatrist at New York Presbyterian Hospital, was asked whether people are living lonelier because of technology. The host, A. J. Hammer, opened up with the following statement: "Scientists are now saying that we really are tuning people out." He went on to ask Dr. Saltz, "Are people using iPods in place of talking to friends and family? Has instant messaging taken the place of real-life interaction among friends? Is technology keeping us from making friends these days?"

Saltz's response was not surprising. "We're big on multitasking, and we like lots of sensory input; but the problem is that all this input isn't about relating, it isn't about communicating, and it isn't about intimacy."

For me the most important words from her response are the last four. *It isn't about intimacy.* I submit to you that the reason some leavers leave is because they were never really there in any meaningful way in the first place. Friendship in the 21st century has been watered down and

144

marginalized, gutted to accommodate a less committed lifestyle. The fine art of friendship-making is adrift in a sea of communication lite. The communication revolution is not bad in itself. It is the overuse or misuse of the tools now available that hurts genuine friendship. C. S. Lewis mused on this subject: "The ancients believed that friendship seemed the happiest and most fully human of all loves; the crown of life and the school of virtue. The modern world, in comparison, ignores it."[5]

I remember reading the story of an Auschwitz survivor who talked about the way those hellish death camps were void of color. Everything was draped in browns and grays—the buildings, the guards' clothes—everything. She described how she became "color-starved." At first she could not put her finger on what was bothering her. Then it hit her. "I want to see color. I miss red and blue and green and purple; I miss color!" When rescued, her eyes were treated to a smorgasbord of beautiful, brilliant colors, and she wept. I think sometimes we can miss something and not know what it is until one day it occurs to us: *I miss friends. Real friends. Close friends. The camaraderie that comes from having someone in my life who knows me inside out and loves me anyway.*

I do not pretend to have any magic answers for this problem; I can only point it out. It's like waking up to realize you have been living on TV dinners when steak was available. Or drinking cheap coffee when you could have had Starbucks. Or driving a run-down Chevy when the keys to a Cadillac are in the drawer. Once you realize this, it is time to take some steps. Determine that you will not settle for "friendship lite." Decide that you will experience the brilliant colors of true friendship. Risk rejection. Reach out and do not expect everything to come to you. Be friendly. And do not ditch someone the first time you ask yourself, "What is this?" Remember, he or she could be manna, a blessing in disguise. Friendship is a two-way street. Cultivate patience and loyalty. Make the effort to keep the friendship alive; stay for the long haul.

Excuse me, but I think I just received an instant message from my newest friendini. Or is that my Blackberry? Sorry to have to run, but hopefully I will see you in the next chapter as we discuss fair-weather friends.

9

BRAINWASHED

Do not conform any longer to the pattern of this world,
but be transformed by the renewing of your mind.

Romans 12:2, NIV

I first met Marjorie when I attended a home Bible study
during the Jesus movement of the '70s. You might say
she became a mother figure to me and to many others
during a time when many of us were struggling to get out
of the destructive lifestyle of the hippie drug culture. She
would prove to be a dear friend of mine for many years to
come. Marjorie had founded a home for unwed mothers,
the outcast and disenfranchised, who really had nowhere
else to go except the streets or jail. Marjorie took them
in before the state put them away. By the time she died,
scores had been healed and restored to a normal, productive life.

But Marjorie's life would have been very different had
She not had a friend who refused to leave. You see, Marjorie
had at one time been a hard-core alcoholic, living to drink

and drinking to live; accustomed to waking up in strange beds with strange men, her life a blur of lost jobs, lost relationships and lost hope. Then one day, in desperation, she attended a church service and gave her heart to Christ. This was a very big deal, for Marjorie was quite well-known for her lifestyle. Those who knew her spread the word that Marjorie the drunk had gotten saved.

Meanwhile, the pastor of the church she was attending became her friend. Over time she poured out her heart to him about her past, sharing her struggles and details of her broken life. All signs pointed to Marjorie being on the mend. One day her pastor friend asked if she might be up to sharing her testimony. "Are you ready?" he asked, searching her eyes. Touched, Marjorie agreed. Floating home, she thought, *Me! Marjorie! Giving my testimony in a church!* For the first time in a very long time, she felt a sliver of self-respect shining in her soul.

She was to speak on a Sunday night, and when the time arrived, the church was full, everyone buzzing about hearing the testimony of Marjorie the alcoholic. But Marjorie never showed. The time came and went. The pastor did his best to make all the excuses he could, hoping she would walk in late, but it was not to be.

Later that evening, asleep in a drunken stupor on her couch, Marjorie thought she heard some kind of loud noise from far away. The sound grew louder and louder. *Knock! Knock! Knock!* She opened her eyes and squinted, trying to focus on the clock. Eight-thirty. Then she remembered. *The church! My testimony!* Her head still spinning, she heard a familiar voice from behind her door. Panicked, she mumbled, "Who is it?"

"It's me, Marjorie. Open up!" her pastor's voice rang in her ears. Ashamed and shaken, she slowly made her way to the door and let him in. Having gone without a drink for several months, she had caved in under the pressure of speaking, the telltale whiskey bottle lying on the floor next to her couch. Fully expecting to be verbally scathed by an indignant man of God for her abysmal failure, she was shocked to hear, "Marjorie, it's okay. God forgives you and so do I." With that he hugged her, prayed with her and left with an invitation to try again when she felt ready.

As Marjorie told me her story, her eyes filled with tears at how her friend and pastor had responded to her failure. "From that night forward, Jeff, I've never touched another drop. It was the unconditional love of a friend in my hour of deepest failure that reached something inside of me and broke the power of that terrible addiction."

Marjorie's story has always stuck in my memory particularly strongly because it exemplifies the power of love and friendship. One negative word from her friend could have been the straw that broke her back. But instead of drowning the remainder of her life in a bottle, she reached scores of desperate girls for Christ. A friend who refused to leave had changed her life.

I have often wondered how Jesus was able to so affect her friend's thinking, so change his character that it was not in him to judge, lash out, reject or scorn her for what had amounted to a huge failure. Instead, he was gracious, kind, merciful and redemptive. Unfortunately, his story is not typical. One of the sort of unspoken scuttlebutts out there is, whatever you do, *do not screw up in front of the church*. The Pharisees who hurled the woman caught in adultery at the feet of Jesus, demanding her execution, can still be found lurking behind the saccharine smiles and pristine edifices of modern-day churches. And, as did their Pharisaical ancestors, they still crucify the fallen.

The Power of a Changed Mind

Something I noticed early on in my own personal ministry was that two types of Christians coexist in the Church—

carnal and spiritual—and these two mind-sets determine the quality of a person's relationships. There are those who would have written Marjorie off as a backslidden hypocrite, a failure who just had not had enough faith to pull through. And there are those whose minds have been renewed to think like Jesus thought.

In his excellent book *The Man in the Mirror,* Patrick Morley prefers to use *cultural* and *biblical* Christians to describe these two different mentalities. Let me explain the difference. Cultural Christians are people who have made a profession of faith in Christ, have probably been water baptized, attend church fairly regularly and are good citizens of their town and country. But as you get to know them, it becomes increasingly clear that it is not Scripture that is shaping their view of the world, of relationships or of their behavior. Their minds have not undergone renewal by the Word of God as Paul admonished:

> Do not conform any longer to the pattern of this world, but be transformed by the renewing of your mind. Then you will be able to test and approve what God's will is—his good, pleasing and perfect will.
>
> Romans 12:2, NIV

There are only two options afforded the Christian: be *conformed* to this world by fitting into its expectations, its ways of living and doing, its worldview; or be *transformed* into the image of Christ by fitting into His expectations, His way of living and doing, His worldview. Transformation into the image of Christ comes only through the renewing of the mind. Virtually all spiritual battles are either won or lost between our ears in the battlefield of the mind.

The process of erasing old ways of thinking and replacing them with a new way of thinking, God's way of thinking, should eventually permeate every area of the Christian's life—relationships, finances, philosophical worldview . . . *everything.* Salvation is only the mere beginning of a lifelong journey of renewal.

This is why Christians should be a *brainwashed* bunch in the best possible sense of the word. Our formerly corrupted, soiled minds must be washed clean by the pure Word of God. For instance, Paul commands husbands to teach their wives the Scriptures, "cleansing her by the washing with water through the word" (Ephesians 5:26, NIV).

This is the unique power of the Word of God. It washes, cleanses and renews the mind of the believer. Cultural Christians somehow miss this. They hear God's Word preached and may read it at home, but somehow it does not find its way into their lifestyles. They still think like the world, and to a great extent, live like the world.

Cultural Christianity is the single greatest problem in the Church today because cultural Christianity produces impotent Christianity: a hollow, symbolic, religious shell of a thing that goes through the motions of spirituality without connecting its adherents to genuine life.

In my part of the world (the Bible Belt), there are three churches on every corner. If you open the yellow pages to shop around for a church home, you will find almost as many pages as you would looking for a doctor or lawyer. I have often wondered why there is no revival with all those churches (I mean *real* revival, not just what someone decides to call revival), why the Church seems so unsuccessful in truly impacting the culture with so many Christians running around. I believe part of the reason is cultural Christianity. Patrick Morley describes a cultural Christian this way:

> Cultural Christianity means to pursue the God we want instead of the God who is. It is the tendency to be shallow in our understanding of God, wanting Him to be more of

a gentle grandfather type who spoils us and lets us have our own way. It is sensing a need for God, but on our own terms. It is wanting the God we have underlined in our Bibles without wanting the rest of Him, too. It is God relative instead of God absolute.[1]

In a moment, we will see how all of this relates to friends. First, let's explore the king of all parables, for it holds an important key to friendships.

A Farmer Planted Seed

When I was called to teach God's Word, I did not have a clue as to how to put together a message. All I knew was to go into the prayer closet (my tiny bedroom), Bible in hand, and ask God to put something on my heart. He did, and the first message I ever brought was on Jesus' parable of the sower found in Matthew 13. Little did I realize at the time how relevant that parable would become in my later years as I watched its truths played out in church life. It helps us understand the two kinds of Christians we have been talking about. The parable begins with Jesus teaching from a boat. "Using the boat as a pulpit, he addressed his congregation, telling stories. 'What do you make of this? A farmer planted seed'" (Matthew 13:2–3).

Jesus later explains to His disciples that the seed the farmer sowed is the Word of God, the Gospel of Christ. He goes on: "As he scattered the seed, some of it fell on the road, and birds ate it" (verse 4). Jesus then says that the seed eaten by the birds represents the people who hear the Gospel of salvation, and before they accept it and are saved, the message is stolen from their hearts by the devil. *These people never experience the salvation of their souls.*

Then Jesus continues: "Some fell in the gravel; it sprouted quickly but didn't put down roots, so when the sun came up it withered just as quickly" (verses 5–6). In this verse,

152

Jesus is describing rootless Christians who endure only for a time; but when hard trials or persecution arise because of their professions of faith, they wilt and walk away, no longer bearing fruit.

Next Jesus says, "Some fell in the weeds; as it came up, it was strangled by the weeds" (verse 7). The seeds among the weeds that become strangled are the people who hear the Word of the Kingdom, but the cares of this world—paying the bills, raising the kids, working on the marriage, finishing that college degree, fretting over the 401(k), along with the deceitful lure of big money—choke, strangle and suffocate the Word within them; and they, too, become unfruitful.

For me, this parable offers a clear explanation of how cultural Christians evolve. The "rootless" Christians just cannot take the heat of persecution. The opinions of men, as well as the fear of loss—in some nations even the possibility of martyrdom—cause them to walk away from their Christian profession. I have personally seen this happen to some very good people for whom I hurt to this day. Walking away from their faith was like trading in a Porsche for a bicycle.

The last negative thing that can happen to the seed of God's Kingdom in someone's life is the "choked" seed. The choked seed represents the people who hear the Word of the Kingdom, accept it and are saved from their sins. They even begin to put down roots and grow in the faith. So far, so good. But then something happens. Read carefully Jesus' explanation of what takes place deep within their hearts:

> "The seed cast in the weeds is the person who hears the kingdom news, but weeds of worry and illusions about getting more and wanting everything under the sun strangle what was heard, and nothing comes of it."
>
> Matthew 13:22

According to Jesus, the weeds of worry and false illusions of the value of material possessions have a detrimental effect on this person's spiritual growth. Jesus' use of the word *choked* literally means, "strangled." His words vividly describe someone who is successfully lured away from what matters most: the Word of God bearing eternal fruit in his or her life. This person has not caved in under direct, heated attack as in the first two cases, but has been lured, coaxed, detoured by an intrusive world. The crucial renewal of his or her mind has been thwarted by distraction. No wonder the psalmist advised us to "meditate day and night" on God's Word (see Psalm 1, NIV).

In summary, Jesus taught that three negative outcomes are possible following the seed of His Word being sown into our hearts. With the exception of the first one, who, as I said, never experiences salvation, *Christians* are the focus. You and I are in the crosshairs of this parable. Stolen away by the devil in stony ground, wilted by fear in shallow ground or choked by worry and illusory pursuits among thorns are the ill-fated consequences of the seed not falling into good ground.

At the close of His parable, Jesus describes a fourth possible outcome for the seed, which represents the biblical Christian. "Some fell on good earth, and produced a harvest beyond his wildest dreams" (Matthew 13:8).

How many people do you know who have experienced harvest beyond their wildest dreams? I know precious few. But this, nevertheless, is the promise of Christ. And this is why our adversary fights spiritual progress at every turn. He no more wants to see a Christian producing fruit beyond his or her wildest dreams than Hitler wanted to wake up in a Jewish synagogue. In explaining this fourth outcome, Jesus says something very interesting. Read closely, because the truth embedded in this verse is the key to biblical Christianity.

154

"But the one who received the seed that fell on good soil is the man who hears the word and *understands* it. He produces a crop, yielding a hundred, sixty or thirty times what was sown."

Matthew 13:23, NIV, italics mine

The one who produces a harvest "beyond their wildest dreams" hears the Word just like all the others. And he or she accepts the Gospel of the Kingdom just like the others. But there is a major difference between them. The biblical Christian *understands* something that the others do not. The Greek word for *understand* means, "to bring or set together."[2] We would call it connecting the dots. The biblical Christian connects two important dots: *hearing* the Word and *doing* the Word. Remember the passages from James we quoted earlier? "Do not merely listen to the word, and so deceive yourselves. *Do* what it says" (James 1:22, NIV, italics mine). Remember that morning mirror in chapter 5?

Hearing the Word of God means to *act* on it. It must wind its way down from our heads into our hearts and translate into day-to-day living. When it is heard and not lived out, cultural Christianity is the result. I am convinced that thousands of professing Christians have become literally anesthetized to Bible truth. Hearing it over and over without acting on it has basically desensitized them to being influenced to live it. Like having a flu shot, the cultural Christian has just enough of the real thing to inoculate him or her from ever catching it. This affects every arena of life, including the kinds of friends we make and are. "For as he thinks in his heart, so is he" (Proverbs 23:7, AMPLIFIED).

Cultural or Biblical Friends

In our world, which the Bible calls "godless," broken people living in spiritual darkness relate to other broken people also living in darkness. Relationships are conducted accordingly, as best they know how. No supernatural Spirit has poured God's love into their hearts as Christians have experienced. "God has poured out his love into our hearts by the Holy Spirit, whom he has given us" (Romans 5:5, NIV). They live under no commandment to practice the God-kind of love toward others as does the Christian. Their fallen natures have not been transformed through the miracle of a new birth. They are yet under the sway and spell of sin's power, which only breeds death. Hence, worldly relationships are fraught with betrayal, selfishness, fear and failure. As Carole King so aptly put it, "People can be so cold. They'll hurt you and desert you."

Because Christians have experienced all of the above, the way we treat other people should be different from that of the godless world. There should be a difference with the redeemed—not perfection, but a recognizable difference. The inward life of the believer should influence the *way* we do friendship. It is enlightening to see the extent to which the New Testament addresses the issue of relationships. The passages that deal with fellowship, or, as one wag put it, how we "one another one another," cover the Bible landscape.

For example, we are told that our relationship with God is directly affected by our relationships with others. So it really matters how we treat people, friends included. Let me pluck just a few truths out of God's Word that relate to friendships. Notice how much they matter even in the eternal scheme of things.

> *We will be accountable to Christ for how we treated others*: "The King will reply, 'I tell you the truth, whatever you did for one of the least of these brothers of mine, you did for me'" (Matthew 25:40, NIV).
> *We reflect Christ by how we treat others*: "A new command I give you: Love one another. As I have loved you, so you must love one another" (John 13:34, NIV).

156

To either bless or hurt members of Christ's body is to bless or hurt ourselves: "The way God designed our bodies is a model for understanding our lives together as a church. . . . If one part hurts, every other part is involved in the hurt, and in the healing. If one part flourishes, every other part enters into the exuberance" (1 Corinthians 12:25–26).

We are called by Christ to walk in truth and authenticity: "What this adds up to, then, is this: no more lies, no more pretense. Tell your neighbor the truth. In Christ's body we're all connected to each other, after all" (Ephesians 4:25).

We are debtors to God to treat others as He has treated us: "Make a clean break with all cutting, backbiting, profane talk. Be gentle with one another, sensitive. Forgive one another as quickly and thoroughly as God in Christ forgave you" (Ephesians 4:31–32).

In light of these verses, what do you think a Christian friendship should look like? If the acid test of whether God is truly among us is by how we "love one another," shouldn't this be one of the key focal points of our profession of faith? Aside from marriage, friendship is the only arena where these truths can manifest themselves. Keeping in mind that we walk in a covenant relationship with a loyal Savior, who has also promised to "never leave nor forsake us," shouldn't there be a trickle-down effect in our relationships? This is where the renewing of our minds kicks in.

For instance, as I write this chapter I am definitely ticked at a longtime friend. He really bungled some things that meant a lot to me, and I, frankly, do not know what to say to him. But here's the rub. I cannot just say, "Well, you really let me down. So, *adios, amigo!* Thanks for the memories. Hate to go, but you just shouldn't have done that. Have a great life!"

It would be nice if it was that easy, but it is not. The full weight of all that biblical Christianity represents is sitting on my shoulders like an eight-hundred-pound gorilla. The Holy Spirit, who lives in my heart, is already bugging me about calling him to talk the matter over. He is my friend, and though I could thrash him soundly with a wet noodle for what he did, Jesus says *work it out*. If I were to walk away, the first Adam will have won the day. To work it through to restoration is to submit to Christ, the last Adam, and bring Him glory in the world.

When Christian friends work through conflict, experiencing peace and resolution, the godless world is afforded a glimpse of the heavenly Father. A recent poll by Baylor University and the Gallup Organization discovered that people viewed God four different ways: angry, benevolent, critical and distant.[3] With such a negative view of God out there, our skeptical world needs to see modeled before them the true nature of love that God actually represents.

A big part of the problem is that I, for one, am selfish to the core. And that is one of the reasons relationships in my life experience trouble. If not for the upward tug of the Scriptures, it would all be about *me*; meeting my needs, doing what *I* want to do. I really think that most of the time the devil does not have to do a whole lot in my case. He is not my most consistent enemy. Jeff is; that is, the first Adam in Jeff. No wonder Jesus said that we each would have to pick up our cross on a daily basis to even think about successfully following Him.

Look around you at all the relational frustration and disappointment. We want great friendships, we want our marriages to work, we have the best of intentions in our attempts to successfully relate, but we are flawed. When sin entered our world, the people we were supposed to be were shattered; we were fractured by the sin nature the day we were born. David admitted, "I was born in sin, shaped in iniquity" (see Psalm 51:5). There is no greater evidence of sin's horrific damage than in our relationships, with both God and each other.

This is why our minds *must* be renewed. We desperately need our worldly, ungodly concepts of love and friendship to be transformed by God's Word. Otherwise it will remain all about us, and this attitude brands "D.O.A." on any relationship. There is a reason the middle letter in sin is "I."

Then how do we do this? How does one renew his or her mind? How can you erase old ways of thinking and replace them with new ways? For me, the prime time to renew my mind is in the presence of conflict. Conflict in a relationship can either send you into a spiral of frustration or it can drive you into the Scriptures. When I can tell I am not responding to a given situation in a godly way, as in my conflict with Frank the fireman on the racquetball court, or my current conflict with my other friend, I go to the Bible for answers.

It is sort of like WD-40—you know, the oil in a can, the ultimate squeak fixer. Just recently the chair in my study started squeaking so bad, you could hear it over the phone. So, I just grabbed my WD-40, squirted the trouble area and *voila!* It was gone. That is what Scripture does for me in conflicts. When something starts squeaking in a relationship, I squirt my thinking with scriptural truth. *The first Adam is always the source of the squeak.* Pride, stubbornness, fear, anger, holding grudges—all find their source in the first Adam, the fallen nature. Paul knew this well when he wrote:

> I obviously need help! I realize that I don't have what it takes. I can will it, but I can't do it. I decide to do good, but I don't really do it; I decide not to do bad, but then I do it anyway. . . . Something has gone wrong deep within me and gets the better of me every time.
>
> Romans 7:18–20

When I turn to the Word of God for renewal, I invariably see two things: what I am doing wrong, and how I can do it right. In the frustration of relational conflict, when I have the choice to embrace either the flesh or truth, I choose truth and renew my mind. However, being stubborn, selfish and very inclined to slip back into old habit patterns of behavior, I have to apply the WD-40 of Scripture repeatedly to bring the desired effect, which is permanent change. The renewal of the mind is the process by which we first *learn* the truth, then *do* the truth enough times that it brings permanent change.

Tom, another friend of mine, is a disc jockey. Actually, he is more than that. Tom has one of the top-rated Christian music programs in the Dallas-Fort Worth metroplex. But he does not just play music; Tom shares devotional, inspirational messages that minister to thousands of people daily on their way to work between six and eight in the morning.

When I first met Tom a number of years ago, I was starting a new church in his neck of the woods. He has turned out to be, like Tony and Frank, another one of those friends who heal. We hit it off very well because we think a lot alike and have some things in common, like radio, which I mentioned in chapter 1. By his own admission, Tom has "a great face for radio." When you first meet him, you think, *Is this the guy I've been listening to?* Tom has the kind of voice you think God would have if He were to choose to speak to you audibly; but in person he is kind of short, bald and average looking, with a wonderful, welcoming smile. (I got his permission to say this.)

One day Tom and I were talking in his studio. Surrounded by thousands of CDs and books, it has the feel of sitting in a half-price bookstore that also happens to have microphones hanging everywhere. We were discussing sin and selfishness, and Tom said, "Have I told you my acronym for 'sin'?" I said no. "Sin is 'self-indulgent nonsense,'" he said with a smile.

Then Tom got more serious and started spilling his guts. "Jeff," he said in that born-for-radio voice, "I used to have a major problem with anger. It torpedoed virtually all of my friendships sooner or later and almost destroyed my marriage."

I had not known this. "Really?" I said, perking up a bit more.

"Yeah, it was bad." As he shifted in his chair, I could tell it was an uncomfortable topic.

"You see, my dad was an extremely angry man. When he got mad, you were in mortal danger. He got violent. This is why my mother had to steal away in the dead of night to get away from him. As I grew into young manhood, I carried the same kind of rage. It was something I had learned from him. I noticed that when I would blow my stack in front of people, it seemed to give me a kind of power over them. So I began to use it to get my way."

As he said these things, I was very glad I had not been around back then. To hear that radio God-voice yelling at me would not have made my day.

"So when I got married," he said, "I would yell and cuss and carry on at my wife until I got my way." I could not picture Tom yelling, cussing and carrying on, but I always keep in mind that we all are broken in one way or another when Jesus found us. I was touched by his transparency.

"What did you finally do?" I asked. He said it first involved realizing he was carrying his father's rage. As a Christian he just could not live with the contradiction—saved, but full of rage.

"I began to read verses like where Jesus equated anger and hatred with murder," he continued (see Matthew 5:21–22). "And where Paul talked about not allowing the sun to set without settling anger issues" (see Ephesians 4:26). "This really began to convict my heart, and God began to show me that my anger was sin, 'self-indulgent nonsense.' I finally realized that anger was a condition of my heart and the only remedy was for my mind to be renewed."

"You mean, erase the old ways of thinking, and replace them with the new way of thinking, God's way of thinking; sort of 'erase and replace'?" I responded.

"Yes!" he replied. "That's what did it. And it's made all the difference in the world in how I treat people, and has revolutionized my marriage and friendships. People aren't afraid of me anymore."

As I was knocking our conversation around in my head later that day, a thought struck me. I had just heard another reason why leavers leave. Sometimes, like Tom's mother and so many people in Tom's own life had done, they look for the nearest exit sign because the relationship is abusive and frustrating to the point of misery squared. They are literally driven away because we are still relating in the selfish, destructive ways of the unswept rooms of our soul, still infested with the cobwebs of our former thinking.

Hope lies in the renewing of our minds. We need to be brainwashed, literally, in the best possible sense. As long as you are still breathing, you can change, and with that change will come greater success with friendships.

All of this talk about deceivers and leavers has really put me in the mood to focus on the positive side to friendship. Follow me into part 4 as we focus on those wonderful individuals who cleave; who are loyal, true and Christlike.

PART 4

CLEAVERS

"So help me GOD—not even death itself
is going to come between us!"

Ruth 1:17

10

GOD'S TATTOOS

"Look, I've written your names on the backs of my hands."

Isaiah 49:16

While pastoring my first church in the piney woods of East Texas, I led an early-morning prayer meeting that met each weekday from six to seven. The hardest days to get moving were the winter ones. Who in the world wanted to crawl out from under the blankets while it was still dark outside and old man winter was pushing the mercury below freezing? One morning, while driving down the lonely country road that led to church, I spotted a group of dogs sort of hunkered together in a field just off the road. Their watchful eyes glowed like green coals as my headlights shined on them. *Wonder what they're up to?* I thought. "Probably huddled together to stay warm," I muttered to myself.

It did not really strike me in any particular way when I saw them again the next morning, same place, same time. But by the fourth day, I got curious. Grabbing my flash-

Cleavers

light, I pulled over and approached the shivering huddle of
fur. That is when I saw what their issue had been. One of
their little buddies had been struck by a car and died right
there on the side of the road. They just were not going to
leave his side. It was like walking up on a canine viewing
in their own little funeral home outdoors. You may think
it strange, but I could swear they looked at me as if to
say, "Can you give our friend a decent burial?" That day I
did, and I never saw them again. Their mission had been
accomplished.

I cannot tell you how many times I have thought of that
event when pondering the whole notion of "cleavers," those
rare individuals who are there for the long haul, who do
not find the exit door when you are down, shoot at you
from the shadows when you have fallen hard or inwardly
rejoice at your misfortunes. I am talking about the people
who actually possess the qualities we Christians are always
gabbing about but do not always practice. (From this point
I will refer to those people who cleave in loyalty as "cleavers," not to be confused with a meat cutter.)

Those dogs had illustrated for me such an incredible
picture of loyalty and affection. I have often returned to
that scene in the theater of my mind when faced with the
need to show loyalty, say, toward someone like my deceased
friend, Joe. *If those dogs could be loyal and faithful, sticking
by their friend's side like they did, shouldn't I be able to do at
least as much?* I thought. I refuse to be bested by a dog.

It is funny that one of the great impressions in my memory of that noble attribute called loyalty, that inner quality
that moves a person to stick by you no matter what, sprang
from a group of dogs. But if you think about it, whether we
see it modeled in animals or in human beings, the quality
of "cleaving" through loyalty and courage is a standout
event any time it crosses our line of vision. More rare than
common, it is sort of like seeing a meteorite shower on
a clear summer night. "Wow!" we exclaim. Or, "Look!" I

have been struck in the same way when witnessing love the way God loves. Those who cleave in love and loyalty carry a piece of God.

Once, when my daughter, Julia, was young, I bought her an aquarium. We stocked it with the typical Wal-Mart type fish, nothing fancy, though some were very beautiful. After decorating it with multicolored rocks, fake plants and a little house for them to swim around in, I placed the fluorescent light over the top, turned out the bedroom lights and flipped the aquarium light on. What a sight, and so very soothing, like staring at a placid, blue ocean.

There is no question that I got more out of the aquarium than Julia did. Some of my best thinking was done when I went into her room at night, turned out all the bedroom lights and watched the fish swim around in their little world. One night I started thinking, *They really are a lot like us.* That aquarium was their entire world. It was all they knew. They were utterly oblivious to what lay beyond it: another world entirely. There was a room attached to other rooms comprising a house. And beyond that house lay a neighborhood, city, state, country and world. And beyond that world a solar system attached to an endless universe. If they had known even a little of the full truth, it would have blown their fish minds.

And on top of that, unbeknownst to them, a being of much higher intelligence (me) was watching their every move and caring for them. From time to time this being plunged his hand into their world and moved things around, cleaned it, stirred everything up, then withdrew. And each day the hand dropped food in for them, though they never actually saw the hand do this; the food simply appeared on time. I began to wonder if perhaps there was a division among them—those who believed in the hand, and those who did not.

One night I imagined that they all had a discussion. On one side were the believers, who spoke first. "I've seen the

hand, I tell you! I was swimming right here when suddenly
it was all around me. It picked up our house, moved the
ground around and put in that new plant over there. And
. . . then . . ." Breaking down a bit and visibly shaken, the
testifying fish gathers his wits and blurts out, "And the
hand brushed up against me. I felt it. It touched me. It's
real, I tell you!" Unruffled, the other side, the unbelievers, then put in their two cents. "You didn't see a hand.
It just looked like a hand. It was only an act of nature
that moved the ground and our house and deposited the
new plant. Let's be reasonable about this. You have no
empirical proof!"

As I continued thinking about the hand thing, it occurred
to me that God moves in our aquarium, the world, all the
time in ways we never see. He steps in from a world far
vaster than our aquarium, a world that exists in another dimension, the dimension of spirit. He moves things around,
cleans things up and touches some of the aquarium's inhabitants. Some believe in Him, and some claim not to.
Yet God is faithful to show His hand in a few undeniable
ways that we may recognize what we are seeing is not of or
from the aquarium. There is no question that the greatest
display of the hand of God to take place in our little world
was the day Christ died on the cross. On that dark, bright,
ugly, glorious, evil, liberating day, God's hand plunged into
our aquarium with a message: *I love you so much, I am
willing to sacrifice My Son.* This was the most staggering
act of love our world has ever seen.

They say that there are parts of the ocean that mankind
has yet to visit; they are too deep, too vast and too dangerous. And while we now possess the ability to snap stunning
color pictures via the NASA Hubble Space Telescope of what
is called the Cartwheel Galaxy in the constellation named
Sculptor, 500 million light-years away in outer space, the
universe remains largely unfathomable in its breadth. We
have yet to step to its edge and peer who knows where.

168

Likewise, though I have experienced God's love in my heart for many years now, it is still incomprehensible to me in many respects. From time to time we catch glimpses of God's love poking through clouds of trouble, but to grasp its fullness is as impossible as it is to understand the endless universe.

When John declares, "For God so loved the world that He gave His only begotten Son" (John 3:16, NKJV), the sheer weight of his pronouncement passes by like a speeding train. We see it, but only a blur. Paul, who received so much revelation from God that it required a thorn in his flesh to keep him humble, confessed, "We don't yet see things clearly. We're squinting in a fog, peering through a mist" (1 Corinthians 13:12). Then how *does* God translate His love into something we can understand?

Our best tool in explaining the magnitude of God's love is language, which, frankly, is equivalent to grabbing a box of crayons in an attempt to reproduce the *Mona Lisa*. But it is God Himself who utilizes words better than anyone else via His own Word, the Bible. For instance, the prophet Isaiah, under the inspiration of the Holy Spirit, borrowed a picture from everyday life to communicate the outrageous love of God: "Can a mother forget the infant at her breast, walk away from the baby she bore?" (Isaiah 49:15).

The answer to Isaiah's question is, well, *yes*, a mother *can* forsake her child. Isaiah leaves room for that possibility. "But even *if* mothers forget . . ." Even though it is possible with us, it is absurd to think that God could do such a thing. Speaking through Isaiah in the first person, God promises, as a lover might promise his beloved, "I'd never forget you—never."

This truth rings like a beautiful church bell on a clear, sun-lit morning. *God will never forget you.* It is impossible for Him to walk out, leaving you hanging. His nature will not allow it. A confused, hard-hearted, desperate mother may be able to, but not God. Isaiah next announces just how outrageous God's love for us is: "Look, I've written your names on the backs of my hands" (verse 16).

I recently watched a news story about a well-known celebrity who had her boyfriend's name tattooed on her arm. However, when the relationship dissolved, she promptly had it removed. But not God. We are tattooed on the palms of His hands—*never* to be removed.

The King James Version of the Bible uses the word *graven* in the place of "written." *Graven* means "to mark out, chisel, or engrave." Another meaning is "to cut in or on."[1] The word has the idea of chiseling something into stone, or cutting a form into wood. God, Isaiah declares, has actually chiseled our names into His hands.

This picture of marked hands is interesting. I believe God was pointing down the tunnel of time to the day when Jesus Christ, the Son of God, would stretch out His hands to receive the harsh nails of a persecuting mob. As the Roman spikes pierced the hands of the spotless Lamb of God, your name and mine were represented in those wounds. God was saying, *This is how much I love you. Your sin is fatal. You will perish without the sacrifice of My Son. By His nail-scarred hands you are forgiven, redeemed and healed.* Isaiah predicted this historic event in graphic detail. The first thing he notes is how badly Jesus would be misunderstood. "We looked down on him, thought he was scum. . . . We thought he brought it on himself, that God was punishing him for his own failures" (Isaiah 53:3–4).

The people surrounding Christ's cross on that somber day actually thought God was judging Him for being a false prophet. Ever felt that way? Like no one really understood what you were all about? I have, and it hurts. Isaiah declares that they could not have been more mistaken about Christ. "But the fact is, it was our pains he carried—our disfigurements, all the things wrong with us" (verse 5).

Jesus was disfigured so that our disfigurements of soul and character might be healed; and He submitted to the pain of being misunderstood and wrongly judged so that we, in turn, could be "received" by God's love. And it was *our* own sins, Isaiah goes on to say, that placed Him on that rugged tree. "But it was our sins that did that to him, that ripped and tore and crushed him—our sins!" (verse 5).

It was not only the sins of that first-century mob screaming for His execution, but it was *our* sins—yours and mine—that called out for His death. An old hymn poses the question, "Were you there when they crucified my Lord?" The answer is yes! We were all there. "God was in Christ reconciling the *world* to Himself" (2 Corinthians 5:19, NASB, italics mine).

The *world* includes all of us, for eternity past and eternity future. The cross reached backward and covered the Old Testament saints who had walked and lived by faith (see Hebrews 11:39–40). And the cross reached forward to all who would one day place their faith in Christ for salvation. "He took the punishment," Isaiah contends, "and that made us whole" (Isaiah 53:5).

Like I said, God's love is absolutely outrageous! It is positively mind-boggling and stupefying. The holy, perfect, just, sovereign, all-powerful, all-knowing, everywhere-at-once God took the blame for our sins and the punishment for our iniquities. And in doing so, He made us whole.

This is why, when the resurrected Jesus suddenly appeared behind locked doors to His terrified disciples, He said, "Look at my hands; look at my feet—it's really me" (Luke 24:39). What did He want them to see? *The holes. The wounds. The "tattoos."*

Jesus continued, "'Touch me. Look me over from head to toe. A ghost doesn't have muscle and bone like this.' As he said this, he showed them his hands and feet" (verses 39–40).

Imagine that the room where they were huddled together grew ghostly silent as the risen Christ passed through locked doors and, standing before them, held out His hands for them to see. Squirming in their seats, the disciples stared wide-eyed at the undeniable marks. The full purpose for why He had actually come to earth began to dawn. It was about far more than walking on water, raising the dead, healing sick people and teaching before great crowds. He had come to die for them.

If His love knew no boundaries, if it was so outrageous as to take the blame and punishment for our sins, then *I know He's got my back*. I can rest in that kind of love. Let us be careful not to project the conditional love of human beings onto Him. Everything about Christ exudes loyalty. David boasted, "I once was young, now I'm a graybeard—not once have I seen an abandoned believer, or his kids out roaming the streets" (Psalm 37:25).

As a pastor, I have seen plenty of believers in very distressing circumstances. I have seen good Christian people in need of financial assistance (I have been there myself). And I have seen many others crushed over unanswered prayers and shattered dreams. But I have never seen God forsake even one of His children looking to Him for help. Somehow, some way, He always comes through. You may not always get everything you want (in fact, you probably won't), but He will see to it that you always get what you need. Think about it a moment. If this kind of love characterized Christ, shouldn't there be found reflections of it in the friendships of those who claim to know Him?

The Helper

The other night I was walking my dog through our neighborhood. I love to walk. It seems that my thoughts come together about stuff that I may have been dealing with all day long with no resolution. This particular night was lovely. A cool breeze brushed up against me and Ollie (a little terrier I rescued from the dog pound two Christmases ago). Looking up, I saw a near-full moon face smiling down on us—so bright that I really did not need the flashlight I had brought—casting everything in a sort of ghostly, pale glow. Aside from a few dogs barking in the distance, it was very quiet.

I often use my walks to reflect on what God has done for me, to size things up in my head; where I have been, where I am and where I think I am going in the future. Sometimes my thoughts turn to some of the terrible traps God has delivered me from, and I shudder. I shudder to think of what *could* have been, of what the adversary intended had God not intervened. And more times than not I say out loud, "Thank You, God, for Your faithfulness!"

> TO CLEAVE IN LOYALTY AND FAITHFULNESS IS TO BE LIKE HIM.

Sometimes I wonder what made the difference; that is, how I was able to turn things around when others who have passed through similar stuff have not. Then I remember what it was that made me turn around, look up, keep going against all odds or have hope when there was no reason for hope. It was the ministry of the Holy Spirit in my heart. The Comforter. And that made me think of yet another angle to God's faithfulness. I know beyond all dispute that without the Holy Spirit's aid, I would have sunk like a brick in the ocean long ago.

Jesus, the loyal and faithful One, promised His disciples that, though He would soon return to the Father, He would "not leave [them] orphans" (John 14:18, NKJV). Speaking about His departure, He assured them of "another Helper," the Holy Spirit, who would abide with them forever. I am mentioning this because I want to highlight the utter faithfulness, the cleaving nature of the One we follow. To cleave in loyalty and faithfulness is to be like Him.

Like Christ, the Holy Spirit is the ultimate Cleaving One. Jesus called Him the *Helper*, which is from a Greek word meaning "called to one's side to give aid."[2] Jesus assured His disciples that the Holy Spirit "dwells with you and will be in you" (John 14:17, NKJV). Talk about a cleaver! The Holy Spirit of the living God was not just called to stand next to us but to take up residence *in* us! "Abide" means, "to stay."[3] He does not come to visit; He comes to stay.

Paul juggles this incredible reality of perfect divinity taking up residence in flawed humanity in 2 Corinthians 4. For him, the idea of God actually living in human jars of clay was amazing. "But this precious treasure—this light and power that now shine within us—is held in a perishable container, that is, in our weak bodies" (2 Corinthians 4:7, TLB).

When you think about it, the Holy Spirit is like a sparkling diamond in a chunk of coal, liquid gold enthroned in dirt. His presence in us is a stunning dichotomy. Glory wrapped in fallen flesh. If you think much at all about this, you have to ask, "Why would God do such a thing?" Paul answers, "[So] everyone can see that the glorious power within must be from God and is not our own" (verse 7, TLB). The Spirit of God dwelling in mere human beings is God's method of show-and-tell. Remember the hand in the aquarium? It is such a contrast: eternity dwelling in a temporary tent. It just stands out.

I can vividly recall one of the joys of my boyhood was the sight each spring of fireflies (you may know them as lightning bugs). There is nothing quite like standing in a quiet field after the sun has set and watching thousands of fireflies flash their luminescent glow like a sky full of tiny lanterns. Each time I watched one of these beautiful displays, I would wonder aloud, "How?" How do they do it? Their light does not come from any source of heat. They are not plugged into a socket. How do they pull this off?

This is what Paul contends should be the reaction of a lost world when observing Christians. They should see the light of Christ shining through us and wonder where it came from. And one of the ways the light shines brightest is in how we relate to one another. Next to the cross, this is what people notice most. This reveals the hand of God moving in the aquarium like nothing else.

"All we are is messengers, errand runners from Jesus for you. It started when God said, 'Light up the darkness!' and our lives filled up with light as we saw and understood God in the face of Christ, all bright and beautiful" (2 Corinthians 4:6).

It is sort of like a football game at my house. My wife is not a huge football fan. She would much rather watch a syrupy sentimental movie about someone's romantic entanglements than football. For me that is hugely boring. But we learned long ago to understand each other's differences, so when she turns on a syrupy movie, I just smile and head for a computer game. But when there is an intense football game on that I happen to want her to watch, I have learned a little secret. All I have to do is tell her something about the quarterback and his wife. Something like, "See that guy? He is the quarterback. His wife has quit coming to the games for some reason. No one knows why. But he sure looks unhappy to me."

Now she is in. Because the game has taken on a relationship angle, she wants to know, "Has the news said anything about her? Do they have kids?" She watches all the close-ups of the quarterback now with renewed interest. This single tidbit of relational news has drawn her in. She will never admit it to me, but it is true: If the quarterback has left his wife, been mean to his parents or ignored his kids, she wants the other team to win. It is all about relationship with her.

Believe it or not, that is exactly how the world looks at Christianity. The unchurched are not impressed with big buildings, Armani suits, the size of our congregations or advanced education. They could not care less if we can expound on Greek verbs or bring an eloquent sermon. The lost world Jesus came to save has an innate sense of what is phony or authentic, real or acted, fluff or genuine. By one thing and one thing only will they say, "Those people really do have something I don't": *by how we relate with one another.* If they see love, it impacts them like nothing else. If they do not, they could not care less if our team wins or not.

I bring out all this to highlight the incredible faithfulness of God, and how that faithfulness should be rubbing off on our relationships. When it does, His light is shined into a dark and hurting world, and His hand is manifested in the aquarium. When I stop and think that I am tattooed on the palm of His hands, that I am always on His mind, it sort of renders me speechless. What a faithful God!

Like I said before, the God you worship will determine your behavior in relationships. When we love one another, cleaving in troubled times, practicing loyalty when we get nothing in return, the inhabitants of the aquarium recognize something noble and God-like and say, "Wow! Where does that come from? They have arguments, but they settle them. They offend one another, but they also forgive. They take care of one another's needs and don't seem to live by the principle of selfishness."

Remember that little talk we had about biblical and cultural Christians? Cleaving friends fall into the biblical Christian category, because to remain loyal, true and committed to a relationship reflects the character of Jesus Christ. Webster's defines *cleave* as "to adhere firmly and closely or loyally and unwaveringly."[4] That is what cleavers do. Cleavers love you with no makeup, when you are twenty pounds too heavy, when you cannot find a job to save your life and when you are not on the top-ten list of people invited to the hottest parties. Got any cleavers around as you read these words?

As I read Paul's description of love in 1 Corinthians 13, it is easy for me to imagine he is describing a person, a friend, a cleaver. Let's pretend that love is a real person and let's

176

give him a real name, say, Dennis. Let's further pretend we are describing Dennis to someone else before we introduce him. Keep in mind that these are the characteristics Christians should be reaching for.

"My friend Dennis never gives up. In fact, Dennis cares more for others than himself. I have never known him to want what he does not have. And he is no strutter. Dennis just flat-out does not get the big head, and I have never seen him force himself on others. And you know what's really refreshing? It isn't always 'me first' with him. He does not fly off the handle, keep score of the sins of others or revel in others' misfortunes. Dennis takes pleasure in truth, is very patient with your faults, trusts God always and always looks for the best in you. He never looks back on what he can't change, but keeps going to the end" (based on 1 Corinthians 13:4–7).

Man! we think to ourselves. *I want to meet this Dennis guy!* Me, too. What a great friend someone like that would be! But you know what? That is what a true friend looks like. While no friend is perfect, these are the characteristics of a genuine friend.

Biographies have always been my favorite read. A big chunk of everything I know about history has come through the lens of reading about someone else's life. Biographies encourage me because they offer real-life examples of others who have successfully walked in the truth I am reaching for. For instance, those about Jonathan and David are snapshots of friendship at its best. Let's take a look at them in the next chapter.

11

THE POWER OF COVENANT

The soul of Jonathan was knit to the soul of David.

1 Samuel 18:1, NKJV

Superman

As I mentioned earlier on, one of the highlights of my day as a young boy was to beat a fast track home so that I could catch one of my all-time favorite shows, *Superman*. I was enthralled with everything about him. In fact, he filled my need for a hero, something every boy longs for. The part of the show I most anticipated was the inevitable confrontation between Superman and the constant stream of bad guys. The bullets bouncing off of his chest while he smiled confidently in the shooter's face; ever the victor over evil, always the savior of the lady in distress, the best and brightest hope of the great city, Metropolis, Superman was my ideal. In fact, I wanted to be like him.

I am going to confess something to you. I wanted so badly to be like Superman that one day I pinned a towel behind my back for a cape, climbed up onto our roof, surveyed my neighborhood from the lofty heights of my single-story house and jumped. No, I did not break a leg. But I *did* get a reality check. The fall twisted my ankle a bit. It hurt, and I was brought down to earth (no pun intended). Superman I was not—not even Superboy.

Through the years we have seen, via Hollywood, that the irresistible aura surrounding Superman has endured. Huge crowds flocked to the first *Superman* movie where the late Christopher Reeve took on the mantle of the man of steel. I, too, was there, taking in afresh and anew the sights and sounds I remembered from so long ago. *Faster than a speeding bullet. More powerful than a locomotive. Able to leap tall buildings in a single bound. "Look! Up in the sky! It's a bird, it's a plane—it's Superman!"*

I have often wondered what it was about Superman that so captivated my heart as a boy and has endured all these years. I believe it has something to do with what he *stood* for as well as what he did. Superman lived for a noble purpose. He was utterly dedicated to using his powers to protect and preserve freedom, goodness and the well-being of those he loved. He was unselfish, never once using his super abilities to take advantage of or manipulate anyone. When he stood there, red cape blowing in the wind, tall and invincible, the values he personified were every bit as much a part of his persona as were his powers. While he could have become a monster, Superman maintained the ideals of a saint.

And, like all of us, Superman had a weakness—kryptonite—the one and only substance that could bring down the otherwise invincible man of steel. Somehow in my little boy's brain I knew that we all had weaknesses, we all had our own particular "kryptonite" that could humble us under its power, and this endeared Superman to me even more.

At the time of my Superman fascination, my personal kryptonite happened to be fear. God gave me a very vivid imagination, which can be bad or good, depending on how it is used. One night while watching TV with my parents, a commercial came on about a new movie called *Village of the Damned*. It was about women giving birth to a group of children with highly superior intelligence and psychic abilities. When they started to do something nasty, like making a man crash into a wall by just willing it, their eyes would turn yellow and glow.

This terrified me. It was the most frightening thing my seven-year-old eyes had ever seen. I grew to hate going to bed because I was certain one of them was under my bed, or was going to come walking out of the closet with eyes glowing. Each time the commercial came on after that, I closed my eyes, plugged my ears and made noises so I would not hear it. This helped me identify with Superman's weakness, that there was something in his life he could not defeat, something he dreaded. And so it was with me.

The Loss of "Why"

Speaking of Superman's values, sociologists and psychologists have been aware for some time now of the loss of moral meaning in contemporary times. You might say we have lost our moral compass, our ultimate "why" for things. According to one prominent sociologist, we are suffering from the loss of what he calls *metanarratives* or "cosmic stories that for millennia have inspired imaginations, conveyed a sense of identity, purpose, and mission, and beckoned many to lofty moral ideals."[1]

This is why, I believe, people still flock to watch "the man of steel." He exemplifies the very ideals that have been sucked out of our culture by dry, lifeless, unexciting, unchallenging, uninspiring, sterilized secularism. The noble virtues that are personified in the cosmic stories of the past, like that of Superman, are what give meaning to existence and inspire us to reach higher.

For instance, Superman believed in absolutes: absolute good and evil, absolute justice, absolute love and absolute loyalty. Superman, in fact, was a covenant-keeping hero. We knew that he would rather die than let Lois Lane come to harm. And we knew that even though Jimmy Olson, his reporter friend at the *Daily Planet*, got into hot water constantly, Superman would never allow his total demise. Why? Because we knew he had vowed to be there for him, period. He was a hero of honor, a man of his word. Never the show-off, every heroic act he performed was done to serve the ideals of love, courage, sacrifice and loyalty. These are the qualities that inspire the human heart. And this is the essence of the attractiveness surrounding Superman.

Jesus, a real, true, historical person, also possessed an irresistible personality. We know from the prophet Isaiah that He was not physically attractive, unlike the blond-haired, blue-eyed Savior seen tacked onto church bulletin boards and depicted in some paintings of Him. He looked very much like a common, ordinary Jewish man. "He had no beauty or majesty to attract us to him, nothing in his appearance that we should desire him" (Isaiah 53:2, NIV). But to know Him was to love Him. To know Him was to wish to never leave Him. Why? Because He personified all that is noble, virtuous and good. People found that irresistible—and still do.

Walking in the kind of friendship Scripture presents, the kind our hearts long for deep down, requires more than the fleeting guidance of fickle emotions. It requires salvaging the old ideals, Superman's ideals, which were really Christ's ideals: the virtues of loyalty, sacrifice, unselfish servanthood and the commitment to live for the good of others.

I believe there is an intense longing in our world to see these kinds of ideals resurrected. We are sick of living a hollow existence in a society gutted of everything that brings meaning and purpose. We want the absolutes worth giving our lives for to be recovered. And there is no better place to start than in our relationships. That, after all, is what the mythical Superman and the real Jesus were all about.

The Bible presents a level of friendship that is based on the same ideals found in our cosmic heroes as well as in Christ. It is called covenant. *Covenant* is found 292 times in the Bible, 272 times in the Old Testament and 20 times in the New Testament. There is only one Hebrew word for *covenant* in the Old Testament, and only one Greek word for *covenant* in the New Testament. The Hebrew word for "covenant," *b@riyth* (ber-eeth), means "cutting," or "compact."[2] Hence, the phrase "cut a covenant." The Greek word for covenant," *diatheke* (dee-ath-ay'-kay), means "a contract."[3] The entire Bible is a book of covenant, beginning with the Old Covenant and ending with the New Covenant (testaments).

Covenant does not depend on feelings, but instead derives its power from commitment. It is not subject to the shifting winds of fickle emotions. Covenant delivers a relationship from the burden of needing to *feel* a particular way in order for it to be valid. We naturally think of marriage when dealing with feelings or the lack thereof, but the same principle of covenant holds true for friendship, as well.

It is not like you and I have to go around making covenants with people verbally. Although that can certainly be done, covenant is an attitude of the heart. It springs from character. It is the way you are on the inside. Because we are broken and flawed through the Fall, we are not covenantal by nature. Most people are opportunistic, not covenantal. We tend to view relationships for what we can get out of them, not what we can contribute. Hence, Paul tells the truth about us when he says, "Most people around here are looking out for themselves, with little concern for the things of Jesus" (Philippians 2:21).

Unfortunately, we live on a covenant-breaking planet, not a covenant-making one. Paul the apostle foresaw that prior to Christ's return to earth, covenant-breaking would reach pandemic levels. Note how most of what he places in his prophetic crosshairs is *relational* in nature.

> Don't be naive. There are difficult times ahead. As the end approaches, people are going to be self-absorbed, money-hungry, self-promoting, stuck-up, profane, contemptuous of parents, crude, coarse, dog-eat-dog, unbending, slanderers, impulsively wild, savage, cynical, treacherous, ruthless, bloated windbags, addicted to lust, and allergic to God. They'll make a show of religion, but behind the scenes they're animals. Stay clear of these people.
>
> 2 Timothy 3:1–5

In contrast to this less-than-stellar character sketch of modern-day man, the God of the Bible is overwhelmingly a covenant-making God. From Noah through the patriarchs—Abraham, Isaac and Jacob—down to David, the nation of Israel, and throughout the New Testament, God reveals Himself as a covenant-maker.

Think about it. Each time you see a rainbow in the sky, it confirms God's covenant with Noah following the awful worldwide flood. "And God said: 'This is the sign of the covenant which I make between Me and you . . . for perpetual generations: I set My rainbow in the cloud, and it shall be for the sign of the covenant between Me and the earth," (Genesis 9:12–13, NKJV). Each time I look at a striking, multicolored rainbow, I am reminded that our God is a covenant-keeping God.

In the Bible, a covenant could be between people or between God and man. Covenants were also made between tribes and nations. In Bible covenants, each party bound himself to fulfill a specified set of conditions and, in turn, was promised certain advantages. A typical Bible covenant involved invoking God as a witness. This was referred to as "a covenant of the Lord," during which time an oath was sworn (see Genesis 21:31; 1 Samuel 20:8). A breach of this type of covenant was viewed as a scandalous sin. For instance, "The marriage contract is called 'the covenant of . . . God.'"[4]

IN TERMS OF FRIENDSHIP, THE MOST OUTSTANDING EXAMPLES ILLUSTRATED IN SCRIPTURE ARE ALWAYS DISCOVERED IN THE SEEDBED OF COVENANT.

Bible covenants were weighty events that were confirmed by oaths and, according to ancient custom, the slaughtering and cutting of an animal into two halves. The parties involved would then pass between the two halves to symbolize that if either of them broke the covenant, their fate would be the same as that of the slain beast (see Genesis 15:9–10, 17–18). Following the time of Moses, the blood of the victim was divided into halves; one half was sprinkled on the altar and the other upon the people. The blood on the altar provided atonement for sin. The blood on the people bespoke Israel being God's covenant people.[5]

Again, I repeat that the god you worship will determine your behavior in relationships. In terms of friendship, the most outstanding examples illustrated in Scripture are always discovered in the seedbed of covenant. If you worship a covenant-making, covenant-keeping God, your loyalty and commitment levels should be far higher than those in a feelings-based relationship.

David and Jonathan

A forest of trees, one poet mused, is hidden in a single acorn. Likewise, a forest of blessings is contained in one godly friendship. The right kind of friendship can often play a huge part in your divine destiny. The friendship of David and Jonathan presents a shining example. Talk about a friendship loaded with divine purpose!

Jonathan was the son of King Saul. We are first introduced to him in 1 Samuel 13:2. Scripture records that Jonathan was a courageous, heroic individual who once led a successful attack against the Philistines with only one thousand men at his disposal. Full of faith and possessed of sterling character, Jonathan was the kind of guy you would want your son to hang around with and your daughter to marry.

Everything began to unravel in Jonathan's household when his father, Saul, the first king of Israel, disobeyed God by refusing to wait on the prophet Samuel to come and offer a burnt offering on behalf of Israel (see 1 Samuel 13). As a consequence of his disobedience, Samuel told him, "Now your kingdom shall not continue. The LORD has sought for Himself a man after His own heart, and the LORD has commanded him to be commander over His people" (1 Samuel 13:14, NKJV).

From here on the decline of Saul reads like a Greek tragedy. His life became marked by fear, anger and the slow, insidious onset of insanity. While Saul spiraled downward in slow descent, an unknown shepherd boy named David had been under the close scrutiny of heaven's eye.

Around seventeen at the time, David, the youngest of the eight sons of Jesse the Bethlehemite, had been put to work at the humble task of shepherding sheep on the back side of the wilderness. Following Saul's disobedience, God had instructed Samuel to go to Jesse's house, "for I have provided Myself a king among his sons" (1 Samuel 16:1, NKJV). As each of Jesse's seven handsome, impressive sons were paraded one by one before Samuel, God said, "Nope, not him." As if it were an afterthought, David was sent for. The Bible provides a brief thumbnail sketch of the next king: "David had a healthy reddish complexion and beautiful eyes, and was fine-looking. The Lord said [to Samuel], Arise, anoint him; this is he" (1 Samuel 16:12, AMPLIFIED).

Just that fast, David's life was forever changed. Providence soon began to move in extraordinary ways. Around this time, Saul began to be troubled by an evil spirit. Desperate for relief, he commanded his servants, "Provide me now a man who can play well, and bring him to me" (1 Samuel 16:17, NKJV). One of his servants just happened to know of David. "Look, I have seen a son of Jesse the Bethlehemite, who is skillful in playing, a mighty man of valor, a man of war, prudent in speech, and a handsome person; and the LORD is with him" (verse 18, NKJV). Who could ignore a résumé like that? Saul sent a message to Jesse: "Send me your son David, who is with the sheep" (verse 19, NKJV).

When the hour to make your mark arrives, God knows where to find you. He found Abraham in Ur of the Chaldees, Moses on the back side of a desert, Joseph in a dark Egyptian dungeon, the disciples in a fishing boat and David on a lonely hillside shepherding sheep. Saul knew nothing of Samuel's visit to Jesse's house or that David had already been anointed to replace him. "And so it was, whenever the spirit from God was upon Saul, that David would take a harp and play it with his hand. Then Saul would become refreshed and well, and the distressing spirit would depart from him" (verse 23, NKJV).

> WHERE ONE HUNDRED MEN CANNOT PLACE YOU, THE PROVIDENCE OF GOD CAN.

The obvious favor on David's life led to Saul's requesting that he live in the king's house. At this time he became Saul's armor bearer. This was a divine setup, backdoor sovereignty, if you will. Where one hundred men cannot place you, the providence of God can.

You very likely are familiar with how everything progressed from here up to the famous conflict between David and the Philistine giant, Goliath. The young shepherd boy stepped into Israel's history books with a sling and a stone. When Goliath's huge frame came slamming to the ground with a rock embedded in his forehead, David became an overnight sensation, a national hero, a legend in his own time. The initial result was positive. Defeating Goliath was front-page material. In today's world the headlines may have read something like:

GIANT SLAIN WITH A SLING!
UNKNOWN SHEPHERD BOY
SAVES THE DAY!
PHILISTINES' CHAMPION NO MATCH
FOR TEEN GIANT-KILLER!

You would think that such a great victory would produce only positive results. But, as is often the case, it instead led to a smorgasbord of repercussions, one of them being jealousy. The women of Israel popularized a song that brought them dancing in the streets: "Saul kills by the thousand, David by the ten thousand!" (1 Samuel 18:7).

Already unstable and deeply insecure, Saul took it hard. Scripture records his reaction: "This made Saul angry—very angry. He took it as a personal insult. He said, 'They credit David with "ten thousands" and me with only "thousands." Before you know it they'll be giving him the kingdom!'" The onset of Saul's paranoia is revealed in the following statement: "From that moment on, Saul kept his eye on David" (verse 8).

David now had a formidable enemy. And it was at this critical juncture in his life that God gave him a covenant friend, one whose help he would come to need more than he could have imagined. As mentioned in chapter 8, God often enters our life by stealth via a person. What looks like a chance encounter may actually be a divine encounter disguised as chance. It was so with David and Jonathan. Following the defeat of Goliath, something very powerful happened in Jonathan's heart as he listened to David speaking with Saul. "The soul of Jonathan was knit to the soul of David, and Jonathan loved him as his own soul" (1 Samuel 18:1, NKJV).

This was not a fleeting infatuation with a charismatic superstar. Jonathan's soul was *knit* to the soul of David. The literal translation from the Hebrew language reads, "The life of Jonathan was bound up with the life of David." *Knit* in the Hebrew language means "to tie," or "knotted."[6] God was clearly behind this knitting of their hearts. Sensing that their friendship held a special purpose, the two men decided to make a covenant. "Then Jonathan and David made a covenant, because he loved him as his own soul" (verse 3, NKJV).

Okay, as a 21st-century male, I have to ask, "Why a covenant? Why not just be friends? What's with the covenant stuff? Why not just say, 'Hey, dude, let's hang around some'?" The answer is simple. They had learned it from the God they worshiped. The God these two heroic young men personally knew was a covenant God. Through Him they had come to understand the meaning and power of covenant.

The steps Jonathan took to seal their covenant are loaded with meaning. He first gave David his robe. Jonathan was heir to the throne, yet he did not hesitate to place on David the symbol of his royal inheritance (see 1 Samuel 18:4). There existed no professional jealousy, no feelings of being threatened. Just trust and affection. Next, Jonathan gave David his sword, bow and belt, a gesture that was highly esteemed in the East, showing great honor. The message behind Jonathan's actions is clear: "This friendship is more valuable to me than the kingdom. What's mine is yours."

Jonathan's gesture beautifully foreshadowed the actions of the Lord Jesus Christ, of whom Paul said, "You are familiar with the generosity of our Master, Jesus Christ. Rich as he was, he gave it all away for us—in one stroke he became poor and we became rich" (2 Corinthians 8:9).

189

Jonathan's actions proved prophetic, too. Soon, Saul's descent into madness began to manifest in angry, irrational outbursts as his hatred of David reached the boiling point. He began commanding his servants to kill David. Another time he attempted to pin David to the wall with a spear. But covenant with Jonathan saved David's life. "Because Jonathan treasured David, he went and warned him" (1 Samuel 19:1). He even remained true when it became clear that David, not himself, would ascend to the throne as the next king of Israel.

Knowing human nature, I can assure you that there were times when David wondered whether Jonathan would choose the bond of blood over friendship. There had to have been days when neither of the two men was flooded with warm, fuzzy feelings of friendship. When a crazy king is trying to kill you at every turn, who can concentrate on a relationship? This was friendship under industrial-strength stress with life-and-death consequences. Everything hell could muster was hurled against their bond. Yet they found security in the worst of times through covenant, and covenant provided their relationship the staying power it enjoyed.

We know where David placed his security when all hell was breaking loose. He placed it in covenant, even reminding Jonathan of their vow during the worst of times. "Therefore you shall deal kindly with your servant, for you have brought your servant into a covenant of the LORD with you" (1 Samuel 20:8, NKJV).

Jonathan also did a little reminding himself, and this back-and-forth between the two about their covenant reveals just how much it had meant, and how much they believed in its power to hold a friendship together. When the two finally parted ways as David was forced to flee the city, Jonathan rehearsed their covenant: "Then Jonathan said to David, 'Go in peace, since we have both sworn in the name of the LORD, saying, "May the LORD be between you and me, and between your descendants and my descendants, forever"'"

190

(verse 42, NKJV). This would be the last time the two friends saw each other. While Jonathan remained in Jerusalem, David found his home in the open fields and dark caves of the Judean wilderness, with Saul always one step behind.

A full decade later, David received a startling message: Saul and Jonathan were both dead, killed by the Philistines in battle (see 2 Samuel 1). In a stunning reversal of circumstances, the former shepherd boy's ascent to the throne became a reality. The covenant cut between these two godly men had survived every possible hellish assault and played a key role in David's destiny becoming a reality.

When I think of David and Jonathan, I wonder how possible it would be for such a drama to be enacted in our day. They say that distance makes the heart grow fonder, but I think more times than not just the opposite happens. How many of us would remain true to a long-gone friend reduced to hiding out in caves, vilified by society, written off by most and whose once-bright future now looked so grim? How easy it would be to forget it all with an entire kingdom at your doorstep as Jonathan had. All of the noble qualities of love, loyalty, devotion and self-sacrifice are not so easily found anymore. Like the mythical Superman and the real Jesus Christ, Jonathan and David were borne along by ideals bigger than themselves.

If the God I worship determines the way I will behave in relationships, then my God had better be a good one. Like I have said, we are broken and flawed by nature, and will not find wholeness apart from our Maker. "For in him we live and move and have our being" (Acts 17:28, NIV). Being able to carry on whole and healthy friendships begins with worshiping the God of covenant.

God hard-wired human beings for worship. I do not care who you are or what you do, you will worship something, because that is what we were *designed* to do. Jesus said as much: "You can't worship two gods at once. Loving one god, you'll end up hating the other. Adoration of one feeds contempt for the other" (Matthew 6:24). Not only do we all worship something, Jesus contends, but we will choose one primary god to worship above all others, being unable to worship two at once.

If you worship self, money, fame or fortune, forget it. Your god will not produce the kind of character we see in David and Jonathan. This level of relationship must be buoyed by something greater. Its source cannot be the shallow wells of our own frail humanity. It must flow from the deeper well of a living faith in God.

It was a gradually dawning revelation for me to realize that the cross of Christ was intended by God to heal relationships in two directions—vertically with Him and horizontally with people. The cross points both vertically toward heaven and horizontally toward humanity. The entire message of the cross is one of reconciliation, one of relationship healing: us with God and us with each other. Why else would He bother to say that if we did not forgive others, He would not forgive us, or that we were to love one another even as He had loved us, if our relationships did not matter to Him?

Before the Fall there were no arguments, hatred, prejudice, bitterness, pride, grudges or selfishness. This all arrived special delivery following the entry of sin into the human race. Jesus Christ came to earth to bring us back to God, true. But He also came to dig within us that deeper well we so desperately need to draw from in order to relate to others.

I once read about a man who was walking down an old country road one morning when he saw something that captured his curiosity. From a distance he could see an old fence post, and, on top of the fence post, something moving. Drawing closer, his first impressions proved true. It was a turtle atop the fence post, his legs flailing away, unable to gain the traction he needed to get down. Of course, the first question to cross the man's mind was, *How in the world did a turtle get on top of this fence post?* After setting the turtle back on the ground, he went home to discover that his son had done it.

I have often thought after reading that story that there are several situations in life that require us to be on top of a fence post, if you know what I mean, and we just do not know how to get there. We know we should love others, walk in victory, avoid sin, live a righteous life, but we just do not know how to get up there. How did that turtle get up there? Something bigger, stronger and greater had to place him there. A turtle could never have crawled, flown or jumped onto it alone. The ability to walk in covenant requires just such a lift. In order for our friendships to enter a new dimension, a loftier place, we need help. Follow me to the next chapter as we discuss the greatest friendship of all.

12

Friends of God

"Now you are my friends."

John 15:15, NLT

One of the classic hymns of the Christian faith celebrates the most amazing friendship possible to mankind. You likely recognize these words:

What a Friend we have in Jesus,
All our sins and griefs to bear!
What a privilege to carry
Everything to God in prayer!

This song and others like it celebrate the greatest privilege we have as Christians—the privilege of being a friend of God. What an incredible thought! Is such a friendship really possible?

The Grand Invitation

Believe it or not, you and I *can* be friends of God. That may seem like a difficult, even ridiculous notion. For instance, the last thing the Old Testament saints thought of when considering God was the word *friend*. Jehovah God was frightening in those days; distant, untouchable—hardly one you would sit down with over a cup of coffee. The writer of Hebrews describes Him in vivid Technicolor:

> Unlike your ancestors, you didn't come to Mount Sinai—all that volcanic blaze and earthshaking rumble—to hear God speak. The earsplitting words and soul-shaking message terrified them and they begged him to stop. When they heard the words—"If an animal touches the Mountain, it's as good as dead"—they were afraid to move. Even Moses was terrified.
>
> Hebrews 12:18–21

Earsplitting words. Soul-shaking messages. Terror in His presence. These descriptions make it clear that to personally approach the Old Testament God was unnerving at best. This was not a God to whom you woke up and said, "Good morning, Friend!" But Jesus changed all that. One can only imagine the look on His disciples' faces when He first referred to God as their "heavenly Father," or when He called Himself their "friend." They knew of only one time in Scripture when someone was called God's friend. "And the scripture was fulfilled that says, 'Abraham believed God, and it was credited to him as righteousness,' and he was called God's friend" (James 2:23, NIV).

The greatest characteristic of Abraham was not as patriarch of the Jews, the father of the nation of Israel, or a great military man who defeated the four armies of the north in order to rescue his nephew, Lot (see Genesis 14). It was his title as the "friend of God" that set the father of our faith apart. Moses came close to it. "The LORD would speak to Moses face to face, as a man speaks with his friend" (Exodus 33:11, NIV). However, only Abraham received the crowning title "friend of God."

If only Abraham was able to attain this lofty place in the entire Old Testament, can you and I really experience friendship with God? Yes! Our hope for it lies in the grand invitation of Jesus Christ to enjoy friendship with Him. "You are my *friends* if you do what I command" (John 15:14, NIV, italics mine).

In all honesty, when I consider the prospect of being a friend with God, something in me recoils a bit. Because this is *God* we are talking about, not just some charismatic leader, good teacher or some other wonderful type of human being. We are talking about the One who hurled the stars into space, spat out the oceans and spoke all living things into existence by divine fiat. He hurls the lightning, Job declares, to the ends of the earth and "thunders with His great voice" (Job 37:5, NLV). My Friend? You have gotta be kidding! How can Someone like that be your friend? At first glance, there is almost a presumptuousness about it.

The invitation to become Christ's friend also forces me to deal with something I have seen a lot of in church circles that has troubled me, so I might as well place it on the table. It is the tendency to humanize God too much, to make Him like one of us, to de-deify Him, treating the Almighty as casually as you would an acquaintance at Starbucks. There is a fancy theological word for this called *anthropomorphism*, which means to morph or change something or someone nonhuman into human. In theology, it is to turn God into a human being. I *do* believe it is possible to become so casual with Christ that one can forget just who, exactly, we are worshiping. In fact, as we discuss this topic of friendship with Jesus, let's be certain we know just whom we're talking about.

First, Jesus was and is God. "In the beginning [before all time] was the Word (Christ), and the Word was with God, and the Word was God Himself" (John 1:1, AMPLIFIED).

Being God, Christ was an active participant in the creation of all things. John continues, "All things were made and came into existence through Him; and without Him was not even one thing made that has come into being" (verse 3, AMPLIFIED).

> GOD NOW HAD A
> FACE THAT SMILED;
> A VOICE THAT
> SOOTHED RATHER
> THAN TERRIFIED;
> WELCOMING,
> OUTSTRETCHED
> ARMS INSTEAD OF
> A LONG, POINTING
> FINGER; EYES THAT
> GLOWED WITH
> LOVE RATHER THAN
> A DISAPPROVING,
> FURROWED BROW.

Look up at the stars while also keeping in mind the endless universes beyond them. Consider the millions of species of created living things. Ask any doctor about the incredible beauty and complexity of the human body, and he or she will only shake his or her head. Then let it hit you between your theological eyes: Jesus, as the second Person of the Godhead, participated in the creation of it all. Before anything was that is, He was there, inhabiting eternity.

This is why the arrival of Jesus Christ to planet Earth was and is so incredibly profound. Here is what happened: The earsplitting, soul-shaking, terrifying God of the Old Testament put on an approachable, human face. He became accessible and lovable, felt what we feel, ate our food, drank our water and walked down dusty, country roads with twelve ordinary, largely blue-collar working men, explaining to them the profundities of life in simple parables they could understand. God the Creator, the magnificent, almighty Jehovah, stepped out of heaven's glory, wrapped Himself in human skin, crawled inside a baby's body and became one of us.

In terms of relationship, the stunning transition from Old Testament God to New Testament Savior was equivalent to someone taking a scroll of Egyptian hieroglyphics and translating it into newspaper-level English. God now had a face that smiled; a voice that soothed rather than terrified; welcoming, outstretched arms instead of a long, pointing finger; eyes that glowed with love rather than a disapproving, furrowed brow. God had needed a translator to stand between Himself and the human race, and Jesus was it. Jesus said, "Anyone who has seen me has seen the Father" (John 14:9, NIV).

When I think of Jesus hanging on the cross, I hear God shouting from the mountaintops, "I love you! And this is how much I want our relationship to be restored." From the moment Christ was born in the feeding trough behind the Bethlehem hotel, God was revealing just how far He was willing to go to reenter relationship with you and me. Talk about sending a Hallmark card when you want to send the very best! I imagine such a card from God, and I think the front may have read something like:

> It's been far too long since we've talked.
> I've missed you terribly.
> The porch light is still on.
> I can't wait to hear from you.
>
> God

On the inside we might find a picture of the manger with the Bethlehem star shining overhead. With the arrival of Christ, the welcome light to God's house now burns bright as the sun.

The entire New Testament is one great big invitation card with your name on it. The God of the universe has invited us to a grand relationship. His invitation has not come that we might embrace a set of stiff, dry rules and regulations that take all the joy out of life. And it is not a call to yet another religion. It is an invitation to a daily, alive, tangible, real relationship with Him.

199

Jesus spent most of His ministry teaching His disciples that He was, indeed, God in the flesh, the awaited Messiah. It is only toward the end, as the crucifixion loomed, that He broached the friendship issue. "I'm no longer calling you servants because servants don't understand what their master is thinking and planning. No, I've named you friends" (John 15:15).

Terms of Endearment

Right before this stunning statement, Jesus laid out His terms for friendship. "You are My friends if you do what I tell you" (John 15:14, NLV). Let me be crystal clear about something. I am not saying that we become friends with Christ by following a set of rules or through our own efforts. To become His friend, we must do whatever He says.

While friendship with Jesus begins with obeying His commands, you must first experience the miracle of the new birth in order to enter the Kingdom of God. "Jesus declared, 'I tell you the truth, no one can see the kingdom of God unless he is born again' " (John 3:3, NIV). Because we were all broken at the Fall and lost our relationship with God, we must be reconciled to Him, not by our own attempts at righteousness, but by coming to the cross for forgiveness. When we ask His forgiveness and turn to Him as our Savior, a miracle happens inside of us. We are born from above. God's Spirit comes into us to live and, in essence, we receive a spiritual heart transplant.

As of this writing, I experienced this incredible miracle 37 years ago as a sixteen-year-old, incarcerated in a juvenile detention center on a drug charge. That night, I prayed with a visiting minister who led me in the sinner's prayer. Having never been presented with the Gospel of Christ before then, I was amazed at how real He became to me. About two years afterward, I returned to that jail, not as an

200

inmate, but as one who wanted to testify to the goodness of God in sending His Son.

You, too, can pray that prayer. Do you know for certain that you have experienced this miracle of transformation? Is there a question mark in the back of your mind when your head hits the pillow at night, all is quiet and you are alone with your thoughts? If so, why not turn to page 211 and pray the simple prayer placed there just for you? Go ahead; settle this crucial question while you are still able.

Now back to this issue of obedience in order to be Jesus' friend. Before you react and say, "I could never perfectly obey Him," remember that there is not a relationship on earth that does not have terms. If you are in a relationship with someone without terms, you are not in a relationship at all. So let's discuss this terms issue a bit further.

First, love is not hindered by terms. In love's eyes, terms are not hurdles to jump over, but happy opportunities to express itself. When Jacob learned that he must serve seven years to win Rachel's hand in marriage, he was more than happy to do it. In fact, the Bible says, "But it only seemed like a few days, he loved her so much" (Genesis 29:20).

One of the first things I noticed happening to me after turning to Christ was a growing affection for Him. I know this may sound a bit wacky to some of you, but it is true, nevertheless. It did not happen overnight. I grew to love Him over time. I knew this had taken place when I took up guitar just so that I could sing worship songs to Him. As I sang I would weep, not with sadness, but out of joy. I can recall wondering if I had flipped my lid, or if perhaps I had fallen in love with an idea, or a philosophy, or just this beautiful historical person. But no, the more I studied the Bible, the more I understood what I was experiencing.

There is no question in my mind that the disciples' motives for following Jesus changed over time. At first they may have been drawn to Him by curiosity. Who was this man who had called them to forsake everything and follow Him? What an extraordinary request! Yet, as the days turned to weeks and the weeks into months, the captivating beauty of Christ's character won their hearts. Hearkening back with a wistful sigh, John wrote about it years later. He writes like a lover recalling his early days with his beloved: "From the very first day, we were there, taking it all in—we heard it with our own ears, saw it with our own eyes, verified it with our own hands" (1 John 1:1).

According to John, the disciples heard, saw and touched Christ. Interestingly, those three words are in what is called in the Greek language the *perfect tense*. The perfect tense is used to refer to a process completed in the past yet still having present results. John penned this first letter as an old man, around AD 90. Though decades had passed since he had personally heard, seen and touched Christ, the experience was reverberating in his soul as if it had happened that day! No doubt about it, to have personally been around Christ was an unforgettable experience. To know Him was to love Him. Even in his old age, John was still dazzled, talking about his experience as if he had just walked away from the Aurora Borealis. Listen:

> The Word of Life appeared right before our eyes; we saw it happen! And now we're telling you in most sober prose that what we witnessed was, incredibly, this: The infinite Life of God himself took shape before us.
>
> 1 John 1:1–2

Christ knew that His disciples were experiencing what anyone getting near Him inevitably will—a deep yearning for ongoing relationship. Knowing this full well, He beckoned, "Want to know how to be My friend? *Obey Me.*" After receiving forgiveness through His shed blood, there is only one way to deepen our relationship with Christ—obedience. So let's be clear about this: The Gospel invitation is an all-

or-nothing proposition. It mirrors our understanding of marriage. In the marriage vows, we swear to be true to our mates, "leaving all others and cleaving only to them, so long as we both shall live." It is just that way with Christ. Remember our discussion earlier on James' comments about not loving the world? Here it is again. "Do you not know that to love the sinful things of the world and to be a friend to them is to be against God? Yes, I say it again, if you are a friend of the world, you are against God" (James 4:4, NLV).

If we are going to walk with Christ, it is either Him or the world, the "world" being the evil world system of which Satan is the prince (see John 14:30). You cannot have it both ways. You will either make friends with the world, or you will forsake the world in order to walk with Christ. The apostle John tossed his hat in the same ring when he said, "Don't love the world's ways. Don't love the world's goods. Love of the world squeezes out love for the Father" (1 John 2:15).

When you think about it, this only makes sense. Let's imagine for a moment that the evil, godless world out there were a human being we are considering befriending. What would that person be like? John describes the world this way:

> For all that is in the world—the lust of the flesh [craving for sensual gratification] and the lust of the eyes [greedy longings of the mind] and the pride of life [assurance in one's own resources or in the stability of earthly things]—these do not come from the Father but are from the world [itself].
>
> 1 John 2:16, AMPLIFIED

IF THE WORLD WERE A PERSON, HIS OR HER EYES WOULD BE FILLED WITH LUST. ENSLAVED TO CONSTANT SENSUAL CRAVINGS, HIS OR HER TRUST WOULD BE IN EARTHLY THINGS, NOT GOD.

According to John, if the world were a person, his or her eyes would be filled with lust. Enslaved to constant sensual cravings, his or her trust would be in earthly things, not God. If the world were a person, his or her lifestyle would be in direct opposition to everything Jesus taught. Every move he or she made would grieve the Holy Spirit. The places he or she went would be contrary to any place God would lead him or her to. The person's conversation would be filled with cursing, lies and blasphemy; and his or her philosophy about life would be totally ungodly, prideful and arrogant, characterized by an "I don't need God" attitude. In short, this person named "World," whom you *will* befriend if you do not befriend Christ, would not be someone a Christian seeking friendship with God would hang around with for five minutes!

No wonder James says, "If your aim is to enjoy the evil pleasure of the unsaved world, you cannot also be a friend of God" (James 4:4, TLB). As I mentioned in chapter 2, I can recall that the first thing God impressed my heart to do following my salvation experience was to separate myself from people and things that were not godly. To remain in my sinful surroundings and relationships would have been to cut off my relationship with Christ.

As long as we are talking about hard-core discipleship and a life of obedience, let me be very truthful with you about something. Walking with Christ can sometimes require making some very tough choices. How hard, you ask? Well, that depends on your situation, but all totally committed followers of Christ will have to make some very tough decisions from time to time. Jesus often used exaggeration in order to drive home a point. Here is an example: "If your right eye causes you to sin, gouge it out and throw it away. It is better for you to lose one part of your body than for your whole body to be thrown into hell" (Matthew 5:29, NIV).

Of course, He was not being literal here, so do not go and pluck your eye out if you have looked at something you should not have. What He *was* saying is that sometimes we are presented with very tough and painful decisions;

decisions that will determine whether we enjoy a fruitful, ongoing relationship with God or not. And some of those decisions are painful. In fact, sometimes the right decision can be a gut-wrenching and heartbreaking ordeal.

I am not trying to scare you. It is just the truth. For instance, would you be willing to walk away from a relationship you are strongly attached to if it was causing you to compromise your walk with God? Or are you willing to take a stand for Christ should it cost you your job or the acceptance of your family? Would you be willing to lay down a habit you know is wrong, even if it were to require difficult steps on your part to kick it?

Jesus is making the point that sometimes life presents us with very difficult decisions where, like it or not, a whole lot—maybe everything—is riding on whether we make the right one. Our walk with God, spiritual health, even our calling and eternal destiny can all hang in the balance with some decisions. He is telling us that such decision making will not be easy, but that *nothing*—not a person, not a habit, not *anything*—is worth sacrificing your relationship with Him.

Jesus is also pointing out the exceedingly damaging nature of sin itself. Metaphorically, it is better to lose an eye or a limb than to perish in sin. Better to make a right but painful decision up front, says Christ, than to choose the immediate pleasure of sin, only to experience the multiplied pain of hard consequences down the road.

The message of the New Testament Gospel of Christ is an all-or-nothing proposition. He is either *Lord of all* or *not at all*. This is the reason so many who profess Christ never experience the fullness of life that He promised. It just is not available to those who compartmentalize God by giving Him a slice of their time (Sunday mornings) along with everything else. Sure, we have to function, and God understands all that. He does not ask for all of our time any more than we would ask our spouses to sit and stare at us all day long, telling us how wonderful we are. We only want to be first in their devotion, above all others. And that is what God wants, too.

God is a jealous lover, says James. When we place *anything* above Him, we are reneging on the terms.

> You're cheating on God. If all you want is your own way, flirting with the world every chance you get, you end up enemies of God and his way. And do you suppose God doesn't care? The proverb has it that "he's a fiercely jealous lover."
>
> James 4:4–5

You may be thinking at this point, *Jeff, this is a lot to ask!* No, this is marriage, marriage to the Bridegroom whose earthly bride we are. You and I entered into a covenant relationship when we became His. We are not dating God, which is apparently what some professing Christians believe. The dating part happened when the Holy Spirit was wooing us toward Christ. When we accepted Him as Savior, we lost all of our rights and are now no longer our own. "You were bought at a price" (1 Corinthians 6:20, NIV).

These are the terms of endearment, the requirements of intimacy with Him. The Bridegroom beckons us to enter a relationship with Him so rich that Paul admitted, "Everything I once thought I had going for me is insignificant—dog dung. I've dumped it all in the trash so that I could embrace Christ and be embraced by him" (Philippians 3:8).

Through the years, I have learned that what God does in my life is ultimately for my good, though there have certainly been times I have taken issue with Him. His reason for requiring our full, undivided devotion is for our own good. Let's get that through our thick skulls. He is not being a mean old miser in heaven who does not want us enjoying life. He just has a better plan. "And what he gives in love is far better than anything else you'll find" (James 4:6).

There you have it! He requires our all, knowing that whatever we manage to dig up in our own quest for happiness and fulfillment cannot touch what He has in store. Do you believe that? I mean, *really* believe that? It all comes down to trust, doesn't it? This whole relationship issue with God is reducible to the trust factor. Remember that manna we talked about? *If I sell out to His terms of endearment*, we wonder, *will I be burned in the end, or will my life have been enriched beyond anything I could have achieved on my own?* Paul believed the latter: "Now to him who is able to do immeasurably more than all we ask or imagine, according to his power that is at work within us" (Ephesians 3:20, NIV).

Included in Jesus' great invitation is a second term for friendship with God. We have already looked at it extensively earlier on, but it deserves a final glance. It is found in John 15:17—"But remember the root command: Love one another."

Moses left us the Ten Commandments, but Jesus only one. It was His root command. Three simple words: *Love one another.* What makes this verse so important is that it follows on the heels of verse fourteen, which says, "You are My friends if you do whatever I command you" (NKJV). Again, if you desire friendship with Him, obey His commands. Do not play church. Do not flirt with God. Do not dance around the pool while never jumping in. Be serious about your walk with Him.

GOD'S REASON FOR REQUIRING OUR FULL, UNDIVIDED DEVOTION IS FOR OUR OWN GOOD.

Jesus anticipated His Church taking a costly stand for Him in the face of a Christ-rejecting, godless world and as a result, would not enjoy the world's approval. In fact, He warned that we would be hated by the world, "because you are not of the world, but I chose you out of the world, therefore the world hates you" (John 15:19, NKJV).

By God's grace, I have walked with Christ for several decades now. And I can tell you that the America I see on a daily basis is not the America that existed when I first embraced Christianity. You could never have convinced me thirty years ago that God would one day be removed from our public schools, that Nativity scenes would be stripped from the public square, that it would be forbidden in many major department stores at Christmas time to say "Merry Christmas" and that Christians would actually be persecuted by the secular media, not just ignored. Yet, all of these things are true and seem to be growing worse. With all of this antipathy from the world, the Church is called to be its own best comforter. We are to love one another.

Not too long ago, I was listening to a man's testimony about how much he appreciated his wife. After describing the dog-eat-dog, ferociously competitive, hard-hearted workplace he stepped into on a daily basis, he spoke warmly of the welcoming arms of his loving wife on his arrival home, stating that it made all of the day's pressures fade. The workaday world had been a battleground, but home was a sanctuary. That is a picture of what the Church should provide for its own.

Let's pluck just a couple of examples out of Ephesians 4:32. "And be kind to one another, tenderhearted, forgiving one another, even as God in Christ forgave you" (NKJV).

Kindness. Have you needed any lately? Boy, I have. We all make mistakes. We all stumble and fail. We all have clay feet up to our earlobes. And our halos are tarnished and tilted as often as they are snow-white and straight. Because of this, we all need kindness.

And how about tenderheartedness? If you have ever been around someone hard-hearted, you know what it is to long for a tender heart. *Tenderhearted* is found only once in the New Testament. It means "compassionate, full of pity."[1] It is the opposite of hard-hearted, which is to be mean, harsh and stubborn. Jesus healed out of a compassionate heart. "Filled with compassion, Jesus reached out his hand and touched the man. 'I am willing,' he said. 'Be clean!'" (Mark 1:41, NIV).

And who does not need forgiveness? As a pastor, I have watched helplessly as those who have greatly hurt others have literally begged for the mercy of forgiveness, only to be refused. It is a pitiful sight. To forgive is in our family genes. Our Savior was the King of forgivers! Is it really so much to offer God's people kindness, tender hearts and forgiveness? When we do so, we are saying to God, "I want to be Your friend."

In my friendships with Frank the fireman, Tony the pilot, and Tom the disc jockey, just to name a few, I cannot imagine not showing kindness or forgiveness. Because of who we worship, those things are a given.

Some Final Thoughts

As I type out the last words of this book, I am sitting in my study of fifteen years, kicked back in my chair. I have opened the window to allow in the beautiful weather a fresh fall day has brought. A few brown leaves, batted about by a cool breeze, are twirling around in my driveway, prophets of advancing winter. The sky is bright blue, with a few wispy clouds drifting lazily by in the distance. This is my favorite time of year, a welcome relief from the relentless heat of another Texas summer now passed.

A lot of history resides in this study of mine. Through the years we have lived in this house, a huge potpourri of people have come into my life offering varying levels of relationship, some painful and heartbreaking, others joyful and fulfilling. Acquaintances, casual friends and a handful of best friends have all been part of the mix. I am keenly aware that who I am today is largely a result of having known them, for better or worse. They have all played a part in God's workmanship in me. More than any single thing, it is they who have brought a piece of God into my life, or who drove me into His arms for answers only He would have.

By far the most faithful Friend I have known has been the invisible one. I used to think it such a strange statement from Peter when he wrote, "You never saw him, yet you love him. You still don't see him, yet you trust him—with laughter and singing" (1 Peter 1:8). "How unusual," I once wondered aloud, "that we can love someone we have never seen!" But sitting here in my study, I do. I do love Him. Not perfectly, but sincerely. Without sounding religious, preachy or syrupy sentimental, my prayer is that God will change your life in some special way through my ramblings about both earthly and heavenly friends, and that, if not already, He will come to be your best one.

Answering the Grand Invitation

Dear God, I believe You sent Jesus Christ to die for my sins. I want to respond to Your invitation to receive Him as my Savior. I willingly confess that Jesus Christ is Lord and believe in my heart that You raised Him from the dead. Please, God, forgive me of all my sins, and send Your Spirit into my heart to abide with me the rest of my days. Thank You for hearing and answering this prayer. Through Christ, Amen.

If you prayed that prayer, congratulations! We would love to hear from you. You may contact us through the information given in the back of this book. Our prayers and encouragement are with you as you embark on your brand-new life in Christ.

In Christ's name,
Jeff Wickwire

NOTES

Part 1: The Awesome Power of Friendship

1. Wayne Martindale and Jerry Root, eds., *The Quotable Lewis* (Wheaton: Tyndale, 1990), 232.

Chapter 1: A Friend-Shaped Hole in Every Soul

1. Glenn Van Ekeren, *Speaker's Sourcebook II* (Englewood, NJ: Prentice Hall, 1994), 164.

2. Michael W. Smith, "Friends" (lyrics, Deborah D. Smith), from the album *The First Decade, 1983–1993*, Reunion Records, 1993.

3. Three Dog Night, "One Is the Loneliest Number" (written by Harry Nilsson), from the debut album *Three Dog Night*, Dunhill Records, 1969.

4. "Social Isolation Growing in U.S., Study Says," *Washington Post*, 23 June 2006.

5. George Barna, "Americans Identify What They Want Out of Life," http://www.barna.org (26 April 2000).

6. Lynn C. Giles, "The Effect of Social Networks on Ten-Year Survival in Very Old Age Australians," *Journal of Epidemiology and Community Health* 59 (2005): 574–79.

7. Walter Knight, *Master Book of New Illustrations* (Grand Rapids: William B. Eerdmans Publishing Company, 1956), 237–38.

8. James Strong, *The Strongest Strong's Exhaustive Concordance of the Bible* (Grand Rapids: Zondervan, 2001), 5384.

9. Ibid., 2083.

10. Ibid., 6440.

11. Ibid., 734.

12. Joshua Wolf Shenk, *Lincoln's Melancholy* (Boston: Houghton Mifflin Company, 2005), 50.

13. Ibid., 65.

14. Albert Nolan, *Jesus Before Christianity* (Maryknoll, NY: Orbis Books, 1978), 56.

Chapter 2: Friendships That Corrupt

1. Strong, 263.

2. C. S. Lewis, *The Screwtape Letters* (New York: Macmillan, 1961), 56.

3. H.D.M. Spence and Joseph S. Exell, ed., *The Pulpit Commentary* (Grand Rapids: William B. Eerdmans Publishing Company, 1950), 428.

4. Strong, 219.

5. Ibid., 151.

6. Spence and Exell, 228.

Chapter 3: What a Godly Friend Looks Like

1. Philip Yancey, *Disappointment with God* (Grand Rapids: Zondervan, 1997), 257.

2. George Barna, "Christians as Likely to Divorce," http://www.barna.org (8 September 2004).

3. Merrill F. Unger, *The New Unger's Bible Dictionary* (Chicago: Moody Press, 1957), 1311.

4. Ibid., 943.

5. Ibid., 102.

6. John Cook, comp., *The Book of Positive Quotations* (Minneapolis, MN: Fairview Press, 1993), 89.

7. Strong, 78.

8. Strong, 1652.

Chapter 4: The Great Pretenders

1. Strong, 1856.

2. John Sandford and Mark Sandford, *A Comprehensive Guide to Deliverance and Inner Healing* (Grand Rapids: Chosen Books, 1992), 68–69.

3. John Eldredge and Stasi Eldredge, *Captivating* (Nashville: Thomas Nelson Publishers, 2005), 100–101.

4. Unger, 41.

5. Spence and Exell, 424.

6. Arthur A. Pink, *The Life of David, Volume II* (Grand Rapids: Baker, 1981), 105.

7. Strong, 117.

Chapter 5: Morning Mirrors Tell No Lies

1. Charles Swindoll, *The Mystery of God's Will* (Nashville: W Publishing Group, 1999), 87.

Chapter 6: Crawling through Barbed Wire

1. Philip Yancey, *Reaching for the Invisible God* (Grand Rapids: Zondervan, 2000), 88.
2. Unger, 846–47.
3. W. E. Vine, *Vine's Complete Expository Dictionary of Old and New Testament Words* (Nashville: Thomas Nelson Publishers, 1985), 151.
4. Matthew Henry, *Matthew Henry's Commentary* (Peabody, Mass.: Hendrickson Publishers, 1991), 432.
5. Ibid.

Chapter 7: Why Leavers Leave

1. Les Parrott and Leslie Parrott, *Relationships: How to Make Bad Relationships Better and Good Relationships Great* (Grand Rapids: Zondervan, 1998), 95–96.
2. Marcus Tullius Cicero, *On Friendship, On Old Age, On Divination*, trans. Frank O. Copley (Ann Arbor: Ann Arbor Press, 1967), 25.
3. George Barna, "Born Again Adults Less Likely to Co-Habit, Just as Likely to Divorce," http://www.barna.org (6 August 2001).
4. Ibid.
5. *Webster's Ninth New Collegiate Dictionary* (Springfield, MA: Merriam-Webster, Inc., 1990), 797.
6. Marla Paul, *The Friendship Crisis* (Emmaus, PA: Rodale Publishing, 2004), 151.
7. Ibid., 152.
8. Francis Brown, *Hebrew-English Lexicon* (Peabody, Mass.: Hendrickson Publishers, 1979), 888.
9. Strong, 913.

Chapter 8: Angels in Disguise

1. Strong, 569.
2. Unger, 813.
3. Ibid.
4. The Center for Media Research, "Americans Online," http://www.revolution.blogs.com (15 June 2006).
5. C. S. Lewis, *The Four Loves* (New York: Harcourt Brace Jovanovich, 1960), 88.

Chapter 9: Brainwashed

1. Patrick M. Morley, *The Man in the Mirror* (Grand Rapids: Zondervan, 1992), 48.
2. Vine, 650.
3. Baylor Institute for Studies of Religion, "American Piety in the 21st Century," http://www.baylor.edu/pr/news.php?action=story&story=41678 (11 September 2006).

Chapter 10: God's Tattoos

1. Strong, 1503.
2. Vine, 110–111.
3. Strong, 160.
4. *Webster's Ninth New Collegiate Dictionary* (Springfield, MA: Merriam-Webster, Inc., 1990), 247.

Chapter 11: The Power of Covenant

1. Douglas V. Porpora, *Landscapes of the Soul: Loss of Meaning in American Life* (New York: Oxford University, 2001), 353.
2. Strong, 46.
3. Ibid., 65.
4. Unger, 259.
5. Ibid., 260.
6. Strong, 253.

Chapter 12: Friends of God

1. Vine, 472.

Born in upstate New York, **Jeff Wickwire** grew up in Dallas, Texas, after moving with his family at five years of age. At sixteen, after being arrested for drug involvement at the height of the hippie movement, Jeff experienced a dynamic conversion to Christ.

Since then Jeff has served in many capacities, including prison minister, youth pastor, college and career director, radio evangelist and, for the last 23 years, senior pastor.

Jeff graduated from the University of North Texas and continued his education at Luther Rice Seminary and Tyndale Theological Seminary, where he earned both his master's and doctoral degrees.

He has founded three successful, growing churches. He currently serves as pastor of Turning Point Fellowship in Fort Worth. One of the earmarks of Jeff's ministry has been large numbers of conversions. Thousands of people have been won to Christ through the years.

Jeff is known for his practical, clear and timely messages that "put something in your pocket you can carry home and use the next day." His vivid illustrations and commonsense approach to Scripture are widely known for making Christianity easy to understand and live.

Jeff currently lives in Fort Worth with his wife, Cathy.

Jeff has written *Making It Right When You Feel Wronged* (Chosen, 2003), *Gossip, Slander and Other Favorite Pastimes* (Turning Point, 2005) and *The Windshield Is Bigger Than the Rearview Mirror* (Chosen, 2006).

For booking and/or product information please contact:

Dr. Jeff Wickwire
P.O. Box 161069
Fort Worth, TX 76161
Email: wickjl@sbcglobal.net

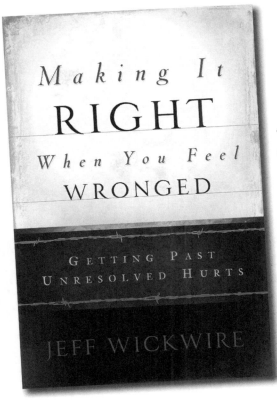

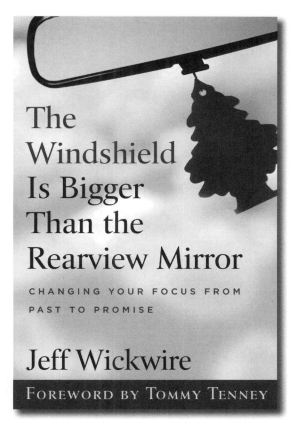

"Getting stuck in the past is one of the most common battles that Christians face—and the enemy revels in it because it distracts us from God's plan. I am confident that Jeff Wickwire will help readers move on and discover the joy that awaits them on the other side."

—James Robison, president and founder, LIFE Outreach International

"The Windshield Is Bigger Than the Rearview Mirror is an outstanding, uplifting book! With humorous anecdotes and wise insight, Dr. Wickwire inspires us to embrace the hope found in our God-ordained vision and to release everything that lies behind that might hinder our pressing on to His perfect plan."

—John Bevere, author, speaker; president, Messenger International

Chosen
Spirit-Filled Living | www.chosenbooks.com